A River A

The Wildlife and History of 'Shakespeare's Avon'.

A journey through the year from source to Severn.

"Sweet Swan of Auon! what a sight it were
To see thee in our waters yet appeare ... "

(Ben Jonson: "To the memory of my beloved, the author
Mr. William Shakespeare, and what he hath left us,"
Published in the First Folio of the plays, 1623)

Mute Swan

Rick Thompson

Grosvenor House
Publishing Limited

All rights reserved
Copyright © Rick Thompson, 2023

The right of Rick Thompson to be identified as the author of this
work has been asserted in accordance with Section 78
of the Copyright, Designs and Patents Act 1988

The book cover is copyright to Rick Thompson

This book is published by
Grosvenor House Publishing Ltd
Link House
140 The Broadway, Tolworth, Surrey, KT6 7HT.
www.grosvenorhousepublishing.co.uk

This book is sold subject to the conditions that it shall not, by way of
trade or otherwise, be lent, resold, hired out or otherwise circulated
without the author's or publisher's prior consent in any form of binding or
cover other than that in which it is published and
without a similar condition including this condition being imposed
on the subsequent purchaser.

A CIP record for this book
is available from the British Library

ISBN 978-1-80381-361-5

Contents

		Page
Sketch Map of the Warwickshire Avon	.. ..	vii
Introduction		1
January: Naseby to Lilbourne		9
February: Lilbourne to Rugby		21
March: Rugby to Ryton Pools		31
April: Bubbenhall to Guy's Cliffe		47
May: Leamington Spa to Warwick		61
June: Warwick to Charlecote Park		81
July: Charlecote to Stratford-upon-Avon		95
August: Stratford to Bidford-on-Avon		107
September: Bidford to Evesham		123
October: Evesham to Wyre Piddle		135
November: Pershore to Eckington Bridge		147
December: Eckington Bridge to Tewkesbury ..		159
Reflections		175

Preface

After moving into the centre of Warwick from a country cottage several years ago, I was delighted to find that a large park alongside the Avon in the centre of town was rich in wildlife. My book, 'Park Life', celebrated the surprising birds, insects, mammals and plants in an urban park. St. Nicholas' Park in Warwick is surrounded by busy roads and housing. But as well as having children's playgrounds, sports fields and a large leisure centre, further upstream there are some fishing pools surrounded by wilder areas of reeds, scrub, mature trees and small meadows. The Warwickshire Avon that flows through the park became the focus of my daily walks. Wherever there is fresh water there is sure to be interesting wildlife.

As the seasons unfolded, the river revealed changing moods. Sometimes it was mirror-calm with fish nosing the surface and wobbling the reflections of the trees and clouds; sometimes the water was languid and lazy, or on a breezy day glittering and sparkling. After heavy rain it could be brown and racing, and occasionally it would surge over its banks to shoot across the surrounding fields as angry flood waters raced downstream.

I began to wonder where these flowing waters had originated and their potential impact further downstream. What were the stories of the settlements that had grown up along the riverbanks at ancient crossing points? Why had the Warwickshire Avon played such a key part in the history of England? And how is the river's state of health? Is it becoming cleaner, or more polluted? I resolved to visit the attractive riverside towns along the length of the Avon, explore their origins, and note the wildlife along the way.

I soon discovered that there's a host of fascinating human stories to be told about the people who lived along the 88-mile Avon valley - some prominent figures who turned the course of British history, others more 'ordinary' who did extraordinary things. So this book includes royal conspiracies, personal dramas, strange folklore, some popular science and even some philosophy. There are also observations on the histories of the towns along the way, the wildlife of the river, and the threats to our natural environment from climate change and from human factors.

Running through my journey along the Avon, like a current in the stream, was the poetry of the writer who was brought up in the Forest of Arden and Stratford-upon-Avon, before swapping rural Warwickshire for bustling London. In his plays illuminating the human condition, he frequently contrasted the innocence and charm of pastoral life with the corruption and violence of the city and the royal court. The Warwickshire Avon is William Shakespeare's Avon, and the path along its route that I followed with visits through the year is called 'Shakespeare's Avon Way'. I hope you will enjoy the journey.

Rick Thompson

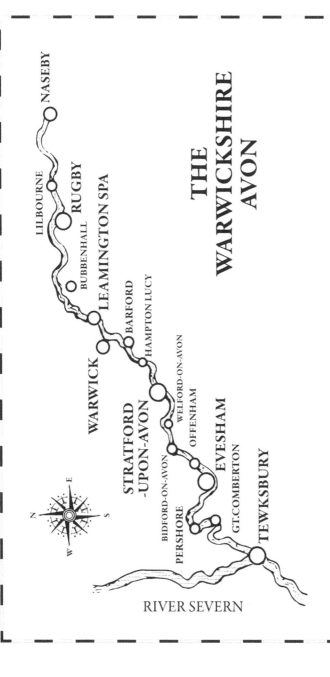

THE WARWICKSHIRE AVON

NASEBY

LILBOURNE

RUGBY

BUBBENHALL

LEAMINGTON SPA

BARFORD

HAMPTON LUCY

WARWICK

STRATFORD-UPON-AVON

WELFORD-ON-AVON

OFFENHAM

EVESHAM

BIDFORD-ON-AVON

PERSHORE

GT.COMBERTON

TEWKSBURY

RIVER SEVERN

N
E
S
W

Introduction

Exploring the River

"Smooth runs the water where the brook is deep."
(Henry VI part II. Act III Scene 1)

Great Crested Grebes

1

The Swan of Avon

It is a beautiful, shining river. But it has a dark past. The Warwickshire Avon, known as 'Shakespeare's Avon', runs through the heart of England like an artery. And over the centuries it has been known to run red with blood as key moments in the nation's history have been played out on its banks in vicious battles for the throne.

Now the Avon is much more tranquil. 'Smooth runs the water'. Instead of gory battles on its banks, the river is known for its leisure pursuits and for its wildlife, with nature reserves dotted along its path, and many different habitats along its 88-mile length from source to Severn. I live in Warwick, the county town lying at the very centre of the Avon valley, half way between its origins as a trickle rising in a village in Northamptonshire to its confluence in Gloucestershire with the longest river in England, the Severn.

There are five River Avons in England, three in Scotland and one in Wales. Why? Because in the Celtic tongue of the Ancient Britons, 'abona' - or in modern Welsh 'afon' - means river. The name is a pleonasm. It's a type of tautology. The River River! It's the same for the River Ouse. There are four Ouses in England. In Celtic, 'usa' simply meant wetness or water.

The Avon that meanders through the midlands was the river of our greatest writer, William Shakespeare, and the waymarked walk along its length is known as 'Shakespeare's Avon Way'. There are little silhouettes of his portrait on the signposts. The dramatist became known as 'The Swan of Avon', a title invented by his contemporary and admirer, Ben Jonson, in a poem he wrote in the First Folio of Shakespeare's plays. The phrase refers to the many mute swans on the River Avon at Stratford where Shakespeare was born, but also to the ancient Greek belief that the souls of poets pass into swans.

In fact the Warwickshire Avon carries just as many stories from history as those dramatised by Bill the Bard. We can discover the tale of the foul-mouthed Scottish Earl who seems to have temporarily lost his head, and in a bit of a panic grabbed the bridle of his king's steed, which eventually led to the monarch losing his head literally, and the creation of the first parliament in Europe. A massacre in an arc of the Avon ended the collective power of the land-owning barons and secured the authority of the crown for generations to come. And the banks of the river saw a blood-soaked conflict that was decisive in the War of the Roses. And why couldn't you own a castle if you were a woman? The valley of the Warwickshire Avon has seen many dramas that have helped to define modern Britain.

Origins

If one goes back in time even further than Shakespeare's day, in fact an enormous span of time, the English Midlands was a huge ocean. We are talking about 200 million years ago – a timescale difficult to imagine. It was the age of the dinosaurs that ruled the earth for 150 million years, before being wiped out by a cataclysmic event, almost certainly the impact of the Chicxulub asteroid slamming into Earth. It left a 100-mile-wide crater just off the Yucatan Peninsular in Mexico. The huge underwater pit was discovered in the late 1970s by geophysicists looking for oil deposits. Paleontologists reckon nearly all the large creatures on earth died in the tsunamis and dust clouds that followed the impact. Life on earth had to reboot and start again.

Swimming in that prehistoric ocean before the asteroid strike were fearsome predators with long necks and rows of razor sharp teeth. One of them, a four-metre-long plesiosaur, may have been injured in an underwater battle, or may simply have become too old and slow to catch fish. It sank lifeless into the soft ocean floor where its skeleton gradually fossilised.

Spool forward 200 million years to the early 19th century, and we find Richard Greaves, a wealthy owner of a fleet of canal barges, opening a large limestone quarry at Wilmcote on the north-west side of Stratford. His workmen kept finding ammonites and other fossil remains as they cut out the slabs of stone. But in 1841 they called Mr. Greaves' attention to something a bit different - a row of knobbly vertebrae and a large pointed head with rows of teeth. It was the almost complete skeleton of our plesiosaur. The fossilised bones were carefully removed and presented to the County Museum in Warwick, where a replica now hangs in pride of place - 'The Wilmcote Plesiosaur'.

So when did the River Avon appear? As this ancient ocean evaporated into swamp and then dry land, the tectonic plates on the Earth's surface were moving and buckling, and successive ice ages carved glacial valleys. Geologists have established that before the last ice age, about 50,000 years ago, the Warwickshire Avon was a small river that drained northwards to the valley of the Trent. Then as the earth's atmosphere cooled, possibly due to continuous thick cloud, massive ice sheets advanced from the poles, and in the English Midlands the glaciers blocked the flow of our little river to the north, west and east. With the Cotswold hills to the south, the water was trapped and formed a freshwater lake.

It was 200 feet deep and covered the whole of Warwickshire. When the deep freeze finally ended, the lake water was able to cut through to the south west, forming the present route of the Avon linking up with the Severn. That was only about 12,000 years ago. So the present day Warwickshire Avon is a comparatively young river, a stripling of a stream, green in years; and the valley is green indeed.

A Year in the Life of the River

It's possible to walk the full length of this green Avon valley. 'Shakespeare's Avon Way' follows the river as closely as it can, using existing footpaths and old bridleways, and a few minor roads when necessary. It passes through towns and villages along the route with plenty of opportunity for walkers to take small diversions to explore local landmarks, historical sites or old churches, and to pause at some lovely riverside pubs! Meandering south-west, the route takes in Rugby where the river is little more than a brook, and to my mind rather neglected, and crosses the ancient Fosse Way to wind round south of Coventry.

The river passes through the splendid Warwickshire Wildlife Trust Reserve of Brandon Marsh with its lakes and reed-beds rich in bird life, worth a visit with a short diversion from the path. Passing through the landscaped estates of Stoneleigh Abbey and Charlecote Manor, the Avon flows through the Georgian elegance of Royal Leamington Spa, beneath the imposing walls of Warwick Castle, and on to the tourist Mecca of Stratford upon Avon.

Growing wider with every mile, it wanders through incredibly pretty villages into the Vale of Evesham, famed for its fruit and veg. The river, now quite substantial and capable of flooding riverside properties if it's in the mood, passes through plummy Pershore, beneath Bredon Hill to the imposing abbey town of Tewkesbury in Gloucestershire, scene of another brutal conflict that left the waters running red.

This book follows the course of the Avon from its source to its confluence with the River Severn. It also follows the seasons month by month through the year, covering a manageable section of the river each month. Unless you are much fitter than I am, it would be quite a challenge to walk it all in one go, even if you plan some overnight stops in hostelries along the route – and there are plenty of pubs and guest houses to choose from. So each month we'll cover a seven or eight mile section of the river, and there are always buses to get you back to where you left your car or bike if necessary. I can recommend the *Travel Line* website where you can search for bus services between any two places, and it will show a map with precise timings of the buses.

There is a beautifully produced 56-page guide to Shakespeare's Avon Way, written by Jenny Davidson. It has maps of each section, coloured photographs, and very detailed descriptions of how to follow the route. The booklet is small enough to tuck into your coat pocket. You can order it online at www.shakespearesavonway.org and all proceeds support the Myton Hospices in Warwick, Rugby and Coventry.

The Power of Nature

The coronavirus lockdowns and the restrictions on contact with family and friends brought a steep rise in mental health problems. The number of people with anxiety, depression or loneliness increased significantly, with underfunded specialist social services unable to help them. But it also brought renewed appreciation of the benefits of contact with nature. It's called by psychologists 'exposure to greenspace'. Local walks, footpaths and urban parks became enormously important for our physical and mental wellbeing, particularly for the 80% of us who live in towns and cities. The internet and newspapers were suddenly full of features about bird identification and the best country walks, and there were plenty of new 'slow TV' series featuring walking alone and reflecting on life, or angling in beautiful scenery.

I guess we all know that a walk in a natural setting cheers us up. Scientific research confirms this. *New Scientist* magazine reported in 2021 that, 'A growing number of psychologists and ecologists are studying the effects of nature on people's mental health and well-being. The links they are uncovering are complex, and not yet fully understood ... But the evidence of positive effects from nature includes studies on specific psychological conditions such as depression, anxiety and mood disorder. Access to nature has also been found to improve sleep and reduce stress, increase happiness and reduce negative emotions... it can even help generate a sense of meaning to life.'

For example, a recent study of workers in the Japanese city of Tsukuba focused on the impact of regular 'greenspace walking' on their mental health. The sociologists call this 'sense of coherence (SOC)', which has three inter-related components: meaningfulness, comprehensibility, and manageability. Meaningfulness is the feeling that there is a meaning for life; comprehensibility is the feeling that one can recognize stress as understandable; and manageability is the feeling that one has enough resources to deal with the stress. There is clear evidence that those who were regular walkers in woods and green spaces were less likely to become depressed. A recent study led by King's College London pointed in particular to the benefits of exposure to birdsong. Of course regular walking in clean air is also very good for your physical health, and according to another Japanese study can add up to a decade to your life!

The New Scientist study concluded that parks and connected urban green spaces are a vital amenity for our well-being. As we face the triple environmental challenges of a climate crisis, a biodiversity crisis and a pollution crisis, it becomes more and more important to protect our green spaces and in particular the health of our rivers.

So join me as the seasons unfold through the year, observing the wildlife along the Warwickshire Avon in the centre of England, spotting some surprising rarities, and reflecting on the extraordinary stories that have unfolded on its banks and the remarkable people who have shaped England through history.

January

Naseby to Lilbourne

*When icicles hang by the wall, and Dick the
shepherd blows his nail,
And Tom bears logs into the hall, and milk comes
frozen home in pail...*
(Love's Labour's Lost. Act V Scene 2)

Grey Heron

The Source

It is as though a giant witch from children's stories has risen spookily from an underground cave, her pointed hat poking through the grass. But this is a cone made of cast iron, rather like an old fashioned fire-extinguisher painted black.

I'm peering over a wall into the grounds of The Manor House opposite the parish church of All Saints in the village of Naseby in West Northamptonshire. The black cone is embossed with gold lettering proclaiming, 'Source of the Avon. 1822'. So the marker is 200 years old, though the river itself is somewhat older! On closer inspection it is clearly a water feature, with a spout for the spring-water to emerge into a dish. Unfortunately there hasn't been a drop of water seen there for years. The source of the Avon has rather inconveniently moved.

The high ground at Naseby is a watershed, with several springs running in different directions. Flowing away to the east is the source of the Nene and to the north can be found the source springs of the River Ise and the River Welland. The source of the Avon now trickles out of an overgrown pipe in a private garden about a hundred yards further west of the witch's hat marker. I must admit that the start of the Shakespeare's Avon Way is far from impressive, especially in mid-winter when the skies are grey and the colours of the countryside are muted. The first couple of miles is along the Welford Road leaving the village to the north-west. The river is no more than a ditch running away south to join the Naseby Reservoir, an attractive 92-acre lake formed to feed the Grand Union Canal. Popular with anglers, it's stocked with carp, perch, roach and pike.

Naseby itself is an interesting village with a very long history. In the 6th century, the high ground was chosen as a good defensive position by a Saxon earl called Hnaef. He built a small fort or burgh, so the settlement was called 'Hnaefes-Burgh'. By the time of the Domesday Book five hundred years later, the name had evolved into 'Navesberie' and later became Navesby, Nathesby and eventually Naseby. By the Middle Ages it had become a substantial market town, but in 1349 it was devastated by The Black Death and much of it was abandoned. The remains of former buildings and lanes can be traced in some of the fields nearby.

So far it has been another mild winter, with no sign of the great snowstorms I can remember from my youth. Certainly the bitter cold winters of Shakespeare's time, with milk brought home frozen and fairs on the ice on the Thames are long gone. There is no doubt that our climate is changing, and at an accelerating pace. It's January, but the song thrushes are in full voice with their sharp repetitive phrases, claiming territory and impressing the females. Wrens are noisy along the roadside hedgerows, scolding any passer-by, occasionally bursting into song, but soon back to work, busily searching for insects, small slugs and spiders. These tiny birds must eat their own body weight every day. At night they huddle together for warmth in holes and old nests. As many as 61 have been found in a single nest-box. They are doing well. The RSPB reckons there are 8 million breeding pairs in Britain. On this cold January day there are plenty of wrens claiming territory with their powerful, trilling song.

A survey by the Wildlife Trusts confirms that spring is indeed coming earlier each year. Many flowers bud and bloom more than two weeks earlier than they did 50 years ago. The birds are certainly pairing up in winter. Beside the path a great spotted woodpecker drums briefly, and a greenfinch is performing its display flight overhead, trilling as it arcs round in wide circles with wings in slo-mo. The first chiffchaff of the year starts calling its name; it's probably a resident bird. More chiffchaffs are overwintering here as the winters become milder.

Shortly after leaving Naseby village, a track to the right leads up a slight incline to a stone monument which seems to have a bowling ball on the top. Maybe Oliver Cromwell was a demon at skittles. For it is the Cromwell Monument marking the Parliamentarian's position overlooking the Naseby battlefield. To the south on a wooded hillock is the 'Windmill Obelisk', a thirty-foot stone spike marking the spot where the king assembled his troops, next to a windmill. The old mill is long gone. The windmills in the valley now are huge modern ones, six of them, with their long white blades slowly turning in the breeze.

Oliver's Army and The Battle of Naseby

It seems to me a pity that this pleasant village is mainly known for a bloody battle that marks a shameful period in British history – the English Civil Wars. But the Battle of Naseby was certainly a crucial event in determining the way England was to be governed for generations to come. There are brown signs on the A14 pointing the way to the battle site with a crossed swords logo. It's difficult to imagine now the impact of the Civil Wars on ordinary people, particularly in the Midlands. One in five men and boys were required to serve in the military. About 4% of the total population of England died in the conflict, that's compared with about 2.2% in World War 1. The Cromwell monument overlooks a sloping field called Broadmoor where thousands were hacked to death in a decisive engagement in the First English Civil War. Information boards show where the armies were positioned and there is a marked trail around the site.

On a foggy morning in the summer of 1645, the main Royalist Army of King Charles I was lined up against the New Model Army of the Protestant Parliamentarians commanded by Sir Thomas Fairfax and Oliver Cromwell. Cromwell has become one of the most controversial figures in British history. Sometimes characterised as an ordinary farmer, he was nothing of the sort. A member of the landed gentry, he converted to Protestantism and was ruthless in the suppression of the Catholic faith in Ireland. In England he was determined to end rule by the King and corrupt Catholic aristocrats in favour of an elected parliament. The Battle of Naseby was to bring to a close the first phase of the Civil War.

Early on 14th June 1645 on the Naseby Ridge, with a blanket of mist below, it must have been difficult for the king and his generals to work out how the opposition was deployed. But as the fog lifted it would have been an extraordinary and intimidating sight. The battlefield front stretched a full two miles, with cavalry on the flanks and the infantry, musketry and bowmen in long lines in the centre. The Royalists were heavily outnumbered by Cromwell's 'ironclads'. Undeterred, Charles ordered his footsoldiers to attack the centre of the Parliamentarian lines and they had the best of the early exchanges. But soon the Royalist lines were broken into smaller groups and some of the trapped infantry began to throw down their arms.

At this point Charles attempted to lead his mounted lifeguards on a counter-attack to rescue the beleaguered foot soldiers. But according to a contemporary account by Sir Edward Hyde, one of the king's nobleman, a kilted and bearded earl described by Hyde as 'a foul-mouthed Scot' single-handedly changed the course of the battle. The Earl of Carnworth grabbed the bridle of the king's mount, swore at his monarch and shouted, "Will ye go upon yir death?" The horse whirled round. The cavalrymen thought that this was a signal to retreat, and withdrew in disarray. Cromwell's New Model Army chased them ruthlessly.

Hyde's account continues, 'The King was pursued by Cromwell's men, who had orders to forgo all plunder and seize only one prize; the monarch himself. At Bloodyman's Ford, King Charles was converged upon and he discharged both of his pistols. The Parliamentarians thought they had him. But the King, a first-class rider, spurred his horse through his hunters and escaped. Carnworth, that profane and undead peer, had single-handedly wounded the King's cause'.

He certainly had. The main Royalist military force was shattered at Naseby and within a year the Parliamentarians had mopped up the last pockets of Royalist resistance. The victors expected Charles to continue as king with substantially reduced powers, but the monarch stubbornly refused all terms and in 1648 the Second Civil War brought about the total defeat of all his supporters. This time the victors showed no mercy. Charles was convicted of high treason and on January 30th 1649 he was beheaded on a scaffold in front of the Palace of Whitehall. Who would have guessed at the time that only eleven years later, by popular demand, the monarchy would be restored with the coronation of Charles II. Those who had executed his father were themselves either executed or given life imprisonment.

Historic Routes

Beyond Naseby, Shakespeare's Avon Way crosses the A5 with the young river about half a mile to the west. There are open fields on either side of the lane and views of Welford ahead. Just to confuse us, there are two Welfords on the river Avon. This village in Northamptonshire lies on an arm of the Grand

Union Canal with brightly painted canal boats in two marinas. The river marks the border between Northamptonshire and Leicestershire. The Warwickshire Welford is called Welford-on-Avon and we'll come to that a few miles beyond Stratford.

There are flocks of linnets and goldfinches bouncing across the pale fields and clinging to the thistle heads along the side of the lane. Both these finches are vocal with tinkling and chirping calls, and both are extremely colourful. The male linnet has a pinky red breast, a blob of rich pink on its forehead and a chestnut back. The male and female goldfinches are both richly coloured with crimson, white and black on the head and a brilliant gold wing-bar, easily seen in flight. Little wonder then that for centuries both species were favourite cage birds across Europe - goldfinches for the moneyed classes, linnets for the working classes. The dilly-dallying girl in the music-hall song was grasping the cage of her old cock linnet as she lost her way to her new home, probably having been evicted.

And from the crown of a tall silver birch there's a different sound from the tinkling goldfinches. A high pitched repeated 'tuwee tuwee'. It's a group of siskins, yellow and black striped little finches with forked tails. They move into the middle of the country in winter in small flocks, presumably to avoid the worst of the weather in coastal regions and further north. They are not averse to visiting feeders in urban gardens, so keep your eyes peeled for their bright yellow breasts and black crowns, and keep your ears peeled for those wheezy, high-pitched calls.

Through my binoculars I can see that among this group of yellow birds, there are two that are different. They are paler, more streaked, and flushed pink. These are redpolls – almost certainly the lesser redpolls that breed in Britain. The common redpoll is a winter visitor and isn't so common! Redpolls are named after the blob of red on the brow of the male. Hanging under the birch branches to nibble the catkins, they look like baubles on a Christmas tree.

Shakespeare's Avon Way leaves the road and crosses the infant river on a little wooden bridge. The Avon is no more than a brook trickling between the fields at this point. A snipe darts away from beneath my feet with its 'creek-creek' call as it takes wing, zig-zagging rapidly away before dropping into a tussock of grass. Sportsmen used to say that if you could shoot two snipe with the two barrels of your shotgun you must be an ace marksman. I think that's a rather awful measure of prowess. The snipe is a gorgeous wader, with a ludicrously long bill that can reach the parts that other waders can't reach, and it is brilliantly camouflaged. That's why you don't see them until they break cover right in front of you and give you a start.

The path then links up with another popular walking route - The Jurassic Way. Nearly 90 miles long, this path links Banbury in Oxfordshire with Stamford in Lincolnshire following a ridge of Jurassic limestone. The way is marked by ammonite logos on the fence posts. It's the same band of limestone, dating back 200 million years, that runs south-west from the Yorkshire coast to emerge at the fossil-rich cliffs at Lyme Regis, and the same stratum where our Warwickshire plesiosaur was discovered. Besides the famous dinosaur bones, these rocks are richly fossiliferous, to use the geologist's word, with the remains of a variety of marine creatures that include reptiles, crustaceans, fish and some sea-mammals. But it is perhaps the curled ammonites that are most characteristic of the Jurassic strata. There is always the chance of finding one in exposed areas of rock anywhere along the route.

Our own route down the Avon joins the towpath of the Grand Union Canal linking London with Birmingham. The Grand Union was completed relatively recently – less than 100 years ago - when a series of existing canals were linked up, making it the longest merged canal in England. At first it managed to compete quite well with the railways for the mass transport of goods – slower, but cheaper. But the development of the road network means that the canal is now used almost entirely for leisure. That's a pity. Moving loads by canal uses much less energy than other forms of transport. After all, a single horse could pull fifty times as much coal on a barge than in a cart. And there was no jolting that could damage fragile goods such as the exports from Wedgwood's factories in Stoke on Trent. Perhaps the canal network could be used again as a low cost, environmentally sound way of transporting heavy goods that don't have to be delivered 'just in time'.

Feeding the Ducks

A group of mallard and a moorhen swim across, clearly hoping to be fed. Now here's a dilemma! Do I feed them some of the crust from my sandwiches or should I not? Some people get hot under the collar when they see children feeding bread to ducks and swans. One sweet-looking elderly lady feeds the waterfowl in my local park every morning, with floating pellets of duck food bought in the supermarket. 'Duck and Swan Blend' costs about £2.50 for a 1.5 kilo bag. In fact there is an amazing range of waterfowl treats available online, described as delicious as well as nutritious. (How do they know they are delicious?) So when our duck-lady sees children lobbing slices of white loaf into the river, she starts squawking and flapping like a duck herself. "You can kill them with that stuff," she shouts!

Is that true? The Royal Society for the Protection of Birds (RSPB) says it's fine to feed small amounts of bread to ducks, but people should also feed them sweetcorn, porridge oats, peas and bird seed. "Just like us, birds need a varied diet to stay healthy," says Tony Whitehead from the charity. "Although ducks and swans can digest all types of bread, too much can leave them feeling full without giving them the important vitamins, minerals and nutrients they need. So although bread isn't harmful, our advice is to feed only small amounts to birds." I would add that it is a bad idea to feed mouldy bread to ducks. It can't be good for their digestion. A pocket full of peas, sweetcorn or rice always seems to go down well with the water birds. But a bag of 'duck food' bought at the local supermarket is even better – it's cheap, and a treat for the birds.

A pair of mallard is mating already. The drake repeatedly bobs his head; the duck is impressed. That bobbing is so sexy! She lies down in the water, he climbs aboard and nibbles the back of her head as he does the deed – in about 4 seconds! Then they both wash, he swims round her in a circle, and then off they go, with her close behind the colourful male like a dutiful wife.

Talking to Submarines

From the canal towpath I can see the shining water of Stanford Reservoir to the right. It was built in the nineteen twenties by damming the River Avon to provide drinking water to the expanding population of Rugby. Now it's an important reserve for wintering wildlife, and managed by Severn Trent. You need a permit to get to the perimeter of the reservoir.

Ahead there are views of a large new housing estate called Houlton. It's being built on the site of the former Rugby radio station. For many years the transmitting station was a notable landmark hereabouts, with a cluster of masts visible for miles. At its height in the 1950s it was the largest of its kind in the world, with 57 transmitters reaching most of the British Empire. As well as relaying the BBC World Service, the station sent out morse-code messages to embassies and shipping, some in secret ciphers. In the early 21st century it was still in use, sending coded messages to British nuclear submarines. It is a chilling thought that a typo in a message from Rugby could have launched us into a nuclear war. The site was closed in 2007. I have no idea how our nuke subs are directed these days.

Railways, Roads, and Mini-castles

The Shakespeare Way briefly follows the line of an old railway - a good section of walking but it's such a shame that these branch lines got the chop in the sixties and seventies in favour of road development. To the right is the rather splendid pile of Stanford Hall, dating back to the late 17th century, now the home of the Fothergill family. The Avon flows through its grounds. Our path rejoins the river just south of the village of Stanford. There's intrusive traffic noise now. The way goes under the A14 with its relentless thundering of lorries going to and from Felixtowe docks, then the path takes us under the A1. So stop your ears and march on towards Lilbourne.

The village of Lilbourne is an attractive place, but to my mind is afflicted by the main roads that seems to surround it. To the west is the busy A5. This long trunk route actually starts at Marble Arch in London and drives north-west to the ferry terminal at Holyhead in North Wales, using parts of the old Roman 'Iter II' road, called by the Anglo-Saxons, 'Watling Street'. Despite the modern traffic, there are still reminders of Lilbourne's historic past. To the left of the trail is 'Lilbourne Castle'. Now don't get too excited. It's hardly Windsor or Warwick. It's a large grassy mound – the remains of a motte and bailey earthworks next to the river. Motte and bailey castles were medieval fortifications introduced into Britain by the Normans. The invaders from northern France must have known they weren't exactly popular. So they made homes that were defensible.

These mini-castles comprised a large conical mound of earth or rubble, the motte, surmounted by a palisade and a stone or timber tower. Most of them also had an embanked enclosure containing additional buildings, the 'bailey', connected to the motte. These small castles acted as garrison forts during military operations, as strongholds, and in many cases as aristocratic residences that were the centres of local administration on behalf of the crown. They generally occupied strategic positions, dominating their surroundings, and as a result are the most visually impressive monuments of the early post-Conquest period surviving in the landscape. From Lilbourne, the path leads westwards to Watling Street, crossing from Northamptonshire into Warwickshire, through the village of Clifton-upon-Dunsmore, and then to the first substantial town on our route - Rugby.

February

Lilbourne to Rugby

When daffodils begin to peer,
With heigh! the doxy, over the dale,
Why, then comes in the sweet o' the year.
(The Winter's Tale. Act IV Scene 2)

Daffodils

Signs of earlier Spring

After an icy start, February has become unseasonably mild with the temperature jumping up to twelve degrees celsius. By the middle of the month there are clumps of daffodils along the hedgerows and under the trees by the path. Year after year, the winter months become less severe in the UK as traditional weather patterns are disrupted. But it seems the whole of Europe can get any kind of weather in February. In Madrid, the erratic jet-stream has produced the heaviest snowfall for 50 years, bringing the city to a standstill for days on end.

Daffodils were said to come into flower on March 1st – St. David's Day – but these days they can bloom in early February in sheltered spots. They always look cheerful and according to the famous poem they made Wordsworth's heart dance. But in folklore and legend they have something of a bitter-sweet reputation. In Greek mythology they were the favourite flower of Persephone, Queen of the Underworld. Pliny reckoned daffodils grew on the banks of the underworld river, the Acheron, delighting the dead. The Egyptians often included daffodils in funeral wreaths to cheer up their dear departed, and to this day in Britain daffodils are planted in graveyards.

But they are also associated with unrequited love, vanity, (Narcissus fell in love with his own reflection), and sometimes with bad luck. Poultry farmers beware. If you bring a bunch of daffs indoors before the eggs have hatched, you won't get any yellow chicks. As for the rest of us, don't just bring in a single flower, bring a bunch. Just one can bring bad luck – so they say! Oh, by the way, the whole plant is poisonous, particularly the bulbs. According to legend, Roman soldiers carried them in case they were mortally wounded. Not a pretty thought. But recently it's been discovered that the chemical in daffs called galantamine, in the right doses, can be used to slow the progress of Alzheimer's Disease.

Watling Street

Crossing the A5 - Watling Street - is probably the dodgiest part of the whole Avon Way. You have to be patient until a decent gap appears in the streams of traffic, and cross briskly! The road is straight as an arrow. "Of course it's straight - it's a Roman road", I hear you murmur. Well, not exactly. Archeologists are sure much of it was created by the Ancient Britons well before Caesar and his men arrived. It connected modern Canterbury with London, crossing the Thames via a natural ford at Westminster. Who would have guessed that before the London bridges were built, horses, carts and livestock could have waded through the Thames where now stand the Houses of Parliament? The road was then carved through woods and fields as directly as possible to St Albans, then north-west to the Midlands, fording the Avon, and on to the Welsh border.

It is true that the Romans paved and extended Watling Street, which must have been an incredible enterprise involving thousands of men. The huge effort recognised the road's vital role in the control of Britain, providing the ability to move columns of troops, supplies and even chariots up and down the country at speed in all weathers. And the newly paved Watling Street was the scene of a decisive battle in England's history that took place more than fifteen hundred years before the Battle of Naseby. It's known as 'The Defeat of Boudica' or 'The Battle of Watling Street', and secured the Romans' conquest of England in AD 60 or 61. Historians aren't sure exactly which year it was because contemporary accounts are imprecise. Equally it isn't clear where along Watling Street the great battle took place, but some experts reckon it was right here, east of Rugby near the villages of Clifton-upon-Dunsmore and Hillmorton.

Boudica's Last Stand

The Iceni were the tribe of the Celtic Britons living in what is now Norfolk. When the Romans invaded southeastern England in 43 AD, the king of the Iceni, Prasutagus, did a deal to secure his position by leaving his lands jointly to his daughters and the Roman Emperor, Nero. However when Prasutagus died, his will was ignored, and the Romans not only seized all his territory but humiliated his family. His widow, Boudica, was publicly flogged and her daughters were 'violated'. The Iceni rose in revolt en masse and linked up with the neighbouring tribe of the Trinovantes who hated the invaders with equal venom. Their former capital, Camulodunum (Colchester), had been seized by the Romans who had built a lavish temple there and demanded the locals pay for it.

The rebel Britons led by the warrior queen destroyed Camulodunum then marched on Londinium (London). According to the historian Tacitus, the Roman General, Suetonius, knew he had insufficient troops to defend Londinium and withdrew them. The city was burned to the ground. Boudica and her army then turned their attention to Verulamium (St. Albans) on Watling Street.

Suetonius drew together legions from other parts of the country amassing a well equipped and trained force of 10,000 men. Nevertheless when they intercepted Boudica's forces they were heavily outnumbered, perhaps by as much as ten-to-one. According to Tacitus, Suetonius addressed his legionaries with practical advice. "Ignore the racket made by these savages.

They are not soldiers. They are not even properly equipped. Stick together. Throw the javelins, then push forward; knock them down with your shields and finish them off with your swords."

Tacitus writes that Boudica rallied her army before the battle, saying, "It is not as a woman descended from noble ancestry but as one of the people ... avenging lost freedom, my scourged body, the outraged chastity of my daughters." The magnificent statue by Thomas Thornycroft on a plinth by Westminster Bridge in London shows Boudica in a chariot with her daughters, addressing her troops before the battle. Unfortunately for the Britons, it was Suetonius who predicted the battle correctly. The professional Roman troops stuck together, threw their javelins, then moved in with shields and swords massacring the Britons. Tacitus says 80,000 were slain. It's horrific to contemplate. Boudica is said to have poisoned herself rather than be captured.

Later in our history, after the Roman Empire had collapsed, this strategically important road became the boundary between Anglo-Saxon England to the south and west, and the Danelaw, governed by the Scandinavian invaders to the north-east for more than 200 years. The modern name 'Watling Street' comes from the Old English *Waecelinga Straet*. The Waeclingas (the people of Waecla) were a tribe in the St Albans area in early medieval times. In fact the city was originally called Waetlingacaester - in modern English, Watlingchester.

The Birch

After crossing Watling Street, the Shakespeare Avon Way passes the Clifton Lakes to the right, a series of large ponds stocked with fish. Huge carp are regularly pulled from the lakes by delighted anglers, and ospreys are sometimes seen during the spring and autumn migration periods. Ospreys are gorgeous fish-eating raptors, related to buzzards, but with a claw that can turn backwards to make a second 'thumb', able to grasp a thrashing fish more effectively. The track here is a green path through open fields called Buckwell Lane, with the Avon wandering away in a loop to the right.

It seems like April weather, but carpets of snowdrops are a reminder that it's still February. When it rains the snowdrops close tight-shut like pearl beads. When they mature, and particularly when the sun shines, they open up inviting in the pollinators. Crocuses open and close in a similar way, only the other way up, pointing to the sky. Flowers are also festooning the bare branches of the trees and hedgerows in the form of beautiful long catkins on the hazel, birch and silver birch. These species are monoecious, meaning they have male and female catkins on the same tree. On a tall silver birch I can see the clusters of green female catkins smooth and sausage-shaped, and the thinner, spikier male catkins.

The silver birch is one of my favourite trees. It's a so-called pioneer species, meaning it was one of the first trees to colonise Britain after the last ice age had wiped out much of the vegetation in the English Midlands. That was around twenty-five thousand years ago. As well as being a fast-growing, attractive tree, with its distinctive bark and shimmering leaves, it has many uses and medicinal properties. In Shakespeare's time, the silver birch was known for its sap that can be collected from holes drilled in the trunk in late February or early March when the sap is rising. Early medics and the village wise women would use it as a general pick-me-up when a patient was ailing.

It probably worked because the sap contains betulin and betulenic acid that boost the immune system, and recent experiments have shown it can even help your immune system to recognise cancer cells and destroy them! An oil called Birch Tar can be extracted from birchwood and was used to treat skin conditions and to waterproof clothing. In more modern times, those who made loudspeaker cabinets favoured birch wood because it has a good natural resonance. Let's hear it for the silver birch!

Beyond the hedgerow small thrushes with stripey heads are hopping about in the fields close to the path. Redwings. One is slightly larger and darker than the others. It's a visitor from Iceland – the coburni race. The others, known as the iliacus sub-species, will have come across the North Sea from Scandinavia and northern Europe to spend the winter here. The coburni race of redwings from Iceland usually overwinter in Ireland and Scotland, so it's interesting to see one this far south. Their close relatives, the resident song thrushes, are singing madly and I watch a bit of a scrap in the trees as two song thrushes, presumably males, compete for territory, throwing themselves at each other in a grapple that leads to one of them high-tailing it.

The track takes us through the centre of the village of Clifton-upon-Dunsmore and across a footbridge over the Avon, now a decent-sized babbling stream about 20 feet across. According to dark ages legend, nearby Dunsmore Heath was a hilly area where a savage bovine beast owned by a giant caused mayhem amongst the nearby farms and villages until it was slain by the local hero, Guy of Warwick. We'll discover more about Guy the slayer of the 'Dun Cow' when we reach Guy's Cliffe on the outskirts of Warwick.

Rugby

A short distance further along the river we find the Oxford Canal, and join the towpath for a couple of miles as it passes to the north of Rugby with the river curving close to the town centre to the left of the Shakespeare Way. The river here is slow, green and overgrown with nettles, brambles, buddleia and orange balsam. There is a path beside it leading from the attractively named Riverside Drive. Unfortunately, this section is neglected. The partly overgrown path is covered in litter, some of it rather unspeakable. Below in the slow-moving water is a collection of shopping trollies, a pink tricycle, and the remains of a metal dustbin – a symbol of waste disposal, now itself undisposed waste. No wonder the Shakespeare Way follows the canal at this point.

But here's some good news. Warwickshire County Council has announced the allocation of ten thousand pounds a year for five years to improve local canals and rivers, 'to promote and protect the county's waterways as a rich habitat for wildlife and a desirable setting for residents, visitors and businesses'. It's not a huge sum, but it's a start. And perhaps they might begin with the section through Rugby!

A short detour from the Avon path takes us away from the retail parks and petrol stations on the ring road to the charming town centre of Rugby, the second largest town in Warwickshire after Nuneaton. You'll pass the Town Hall built between 1959 and 1961, a period of striking 'modernist' architecture featuring geometric blocks, straight lines and interesting textures. I really like Rugby Town Hall. It has clear references to the Art Deco styles of the nineteen twenties. But the much-travelled architectural historian, Nikolaus Pevsner, whose guides to the notable buildings of Britain were popular in the sixties and seventies, declared that the building was, 'quite dead architecturally'. I can't agree, Nick. It's got style.

In the centre of town, the Friday market is in full swing with the fruit and veg merchants shouting their latest knock-down offers. And beyond the town centre are the extensive grounds of Rugby School. This is a sprawling estate of 19th century brick and stone buildings with a huge playing field. I note there are several soccer pitches. I think that Webb Ellis of the first-year sixth form would have been sent off within two minutes if he'd kept on doing that picking-it-up-and-running-with-it thing. (Surely that will never catch on).

Some senior boys are out and about at lunchtime. With shirts rebelliously untucked, and eating KFC chicken nuggets and extruded fries, they walk past discussing Pliny the Elder's 'Naturalis Historia'. No, I made that bit up. They were talking about their scores on Minecraft. At the time of writing, fees for boarding at Rugby School are about £37,000 a year.

Our path along the Shakespeare Avon Way will take us west from Rugby to the outskirts of Kenilworth through the gorgeous grounds of Stoneleigh Abbey, once home of the family of Jane Austen's mum, where some unusual birds are sometimes seen on the river. I wonder how many bird species I'll be able to identify during this journey down the Avon through the seasons of the year. I'm tempted to go for an ambitious target. How about a round hundred? Very unlikely, but you never know. There may be some surprising species on the way. So on we'll go, with a manageable section each month, past Coventry and Kenilworth and on towards Leamington and the county town of historic Warwick.

March

Rugby to Ryton Pools

*I am but mad north-north-west. When the wind is southerly
I know a hawk from a handsaw; [a hanser or heron].*
(Hamlet. Act II Scene 2)

Murmuration
(from a photo by the author)

Brindley's Canal

March is supposed to have mad weather, but this year it is still fairly benign – mostly calm with the wind, such as it is, southerly, or at least from the south-west. Hamlet was suggesting to Rosencrantz and Guildenstern that he is mad only some of the time, as though his temperament reflected the wind direction. Or maybe he was faking it all along. Discuss, with reference to other weather-related imagery in the play.

Our route from Rugby continues to follow the Oxford Canal awhile. This is one of the earliest of cuts in the canal age. It was initially designed by the amazing James Brindley in 1772 with the purpose of bringing coal from the Coventry mines to Oxford and the River Thames. The canal formed part of Brindley's grand plan for a 'waterway cross', linking the rivers Thames, Mersey, Trent and Severn. Brilliant Brindley was educated at home by his mum, and started his career as a millwright's apprentice. He was to become the leading engineer of his generation, creating canals that could overcome any topology with aqueducts, tunnels, and locks. This was half a century before Brunel established his enduring reputation. Brindley is rightly honoured in Birmingham with streets and squares named after him, not to mention 'Brindley Place', a shopping and dining centre alongside the attractive canal basin that used to be heaving with barges unloading coal and iron-ore.

Shakespeare's Avon Way passes Newbold Quarry Park to the left. This is a series of former limestone quarries converted into a lovely little nature reserve with pools for wildfowl including great crested grebes. I hope to be able to glimpse the grebes' fantastic mating dance that includes various synchronised moves including the penguin dance, the weed dance when they offer each other strands of waterweed, and the cat posture. It may be just a bit early in the year. But maybe not. All the other birds are madly pairing up. And sure enough, out in the centre of the lake, two grebes are shaking their tippets at each other, bobbing their heads in unison and sitting up in the water to offer titbits of weed.

The lake is very deep - up to fifty feet in places. In 2018 divers explored the deep parts and found the remains of a pram, a motorbike and two cars dating from the nineteen seventies and eighties. No wonder swimming in the Quarry Park pools is strongly discouraged. Before leaving the canal path and rejoining the River Avon as it curls through Newbold on Avon, I can see across the fields the entrance to the original Oxford Canal tunnel. It's now sealed up to prevent livestock from wandering in; but there are a couple of holes in the brickwork - to allow the bats to use the old tunnel. A nice touch, and, I understand, much appreciated by the local bat population.

Limestone Bonanza

The track takes us downhill, under a railway arch to a white metal footbridge over the river. Looking to the left, there's the rather unattractive Rugby Cement Works. Jenny Davidson's booklet mapping the route of Shakespeare's Avon Way says that in 2005, Rugby Cement Works made the top ten in a poll of buildings people wanted to see demolished. Well, in the past 200 years or so, it has provided work for thousands of local families; and it is world famous! Its products are everywhere.

The business started in 1825 as a small family concern. Tom Walker and his son, George, began producing lime mortar on their land near Newbold-on-Avon, exploiting the very fine lias limestone they found there. Their mortar was in demand; George founded a public company in 1870 and started producing Portland Cement. The business boomed. Concrete was needed across the country, and indeed across the world. After a dazzling number of acquisitions, mergers and take-overs, Rugby Cement is now owned by a billionaire Mexican under the corporate name, Cemex.

These days, employing over two thousand people in the UK, Cemex offers a smorgasbord of limestone-based materials including Low Carbon Concrete, Self Compacting Concrete, Low Density Foam Concrete, Rapid Setting Concrete, Flexible Asphalt, Permeable Asphalt, and many more varieties. So if you are walking along a path, cycling or driving, or entering a high-rise building, you may well be reaping the benefits of the high-quality cement produced in Rugby. Well done, Tom and George.

A Ghost and a Poisoner

The waymarked track here goes through the small village of Long Lawford, past the early Victorian St. John's Church. On the other side of the river is the hamlet of Little Lawford and Lawford Hall, which used to be the ancestral home of the Rouse-Boughton family. It wasn't always happy families there. In Elizabethan times, the owner of the estate lost an arm in an accident. After his death, it's reported that 'One-handed Boughton' haunted the house and had a habit of driving round the countryside at night in a coach drawn by six horses.

In the 18th century the Boughton family was so fed up with the one-armed phantom they attempted to exorcise the ghost with the aid of no fewer than twelve clergymen who, it is said, trapped the ghost in a bottle and threw it into a clay pit. But it seems they'd made a deal with the ghost, and it would be allowed out for a couple of hours at night time to continue the rides through the countryside. There were sightings of the coach and horses crossing the fields in the moonlight.

A hundred years later, a bottle was found in a nearby pond and it was thought it could be the one used to trap the ghost. It was returned to the Boughton family. It isn't recorded what they did with it.

There was even more skulduggery in this quiet hamlet in 1870. The owner of the original Lawford Hall, the exotically named Sir Theophilus Boughton, was found dead in his room. Doctors suspected foul play, and his brother-in-law, Captain Donellan, who was married to Theophilus's sister Theodosia, was arrested and charged with murder. It seems Donellan had hoped to knock-off the baronet and inherit the estate through his wife. He was found guilty of poisoning his brother-in-law with 'laurel water', (hydrogen cyanide), and was hanged in Warwick the following year. The family decided to demolish the Hall and move elsewhere in an attempt to erase the unhappy memories.

The Mysterious Hare

The path stays close to the river for the next couple of miles, with wooden stiles leading across a series of open fields. On a low ridge I can see a pair of black-tipped ears sticking up above the stubble, then the arched chestnut back as a hare lollops away. When threatened, it's capable of racing away at up to 40 miles per hour, making the brown hare Britain's fastest land mammal. At this time of year you may be lucky enough to see a boxing match as the 'mad' March hares square up to each other on their back legs and chase one another in circles. In fact it's the females that throw most of the punches, fending off any male that is too persistent or not impressive enough.

Some natural historians suggest that hares and rabbits were introduced to the British Isles by the Romans, but that may be wrong in both cases. According to the British Mammal Society, rabbits were brought in from mainland Europe in medieval times, with warrens providing food for large estates. There is certainly recent evidence that the Romans in Britain ate rabbits, but were they wild animals? The brown hare has been here much longer, with evidence of their remains dating from the Iron Age nearly 3,000 years ago. And they figure prominently in our ancient folklore.

The stories of the hare as a cunning trickster who uses his wits to get out of dangerous scrapes appear all over the world. The American Br'er Rabbit stories seem to have come with the slaves from West Africa. Br'er (Brother) Rabbit is in fact a hare. Wild rabbits didn't spread across America until the mid-19th century, well after the children's stories had become popular.

There is a terrific book by George Ewart Evans and David Thomson all about the legends, poetry, art, mystery and magic associated with this timid creature. 'The Leaping Hare' points out, among other things, that madness and genius have always been close neighbours, and come together in the hare. In many cultures the hare is associated with the moon, and the lunar cycle that in extremis can cause you to be slightly lunatic apparently. In Celtic mythology the hare was sacred to the moon goddess Andraste. And according to the Roman historian Dio Cassius, Boudica released a hare from under her cloak as a good omen before each battle with the Romans. As we discovered earlier, it didn't work its magic for her at the battle of Watling Street.

And as well as there being a man in the moon, there is a hare in the moon! After I had read about this widely-held belief, I studied the waxing moon for several nights, until - of course - there it is! I could suddenly see it. The top half of the full moon has the hare leaping to the right, with ears laid back, and back legs trailing behind.

Unfortunately our wild hares, sometimes seen boxing in the moonlight, are in peril. Humans are not the only mammals to have been struck down by a deadly virus recently. In 2021 it was reported by Diana Bell, a professor of conservation biology at the University of East Anglia, that more than a thousand hares had been recorded as dying from a new 'viral cocktail'. The fear is that a form of myxomatosis has jumped from rabbits to hares.

In 1952, the owner of an estate in northern France, Paul-Felix Armand-Delille, inoculated two wild rabbits with a strain of the myxoma virus, aiming only to get rid of the rabbits on his property. The 'White Blindness', as Richard Adams called it in 'Watership Down', was almost certainly introduced deliberately into Britain and Ireland in the next two years. The wild rabbit population in the UK was to fall by 99%. Populations of predators that feed on rabbits also plummeted. In Spain it was the Iberian Lynx that almost disappeared. Eagles and buzzards declined everywhere.

But just a few rabbits were resistant, just enough for a new population to emerge. Now in central England the buzzards are back, red kites are thriving, and ravens are seen regularly flying across our towns and cities. Even white-tailed eagles are starting to establish themselves along the south coast after a reintroduction programme. But after the bounce-back, the rabbit population has taken another hit. A new 'haemorrhagic disease virus type two (RHDV2)', emerged in commercial rabbit farms in France in 2010 and spread into the wild population and across the Channel. In Britain rabbit numbers have fallen by 43% in the last 10 years.

Now it seems the virus RHDV2 has been found in dead hares showing typical blindness symptoms. Professor Bell is appealing to members of the public to pick up any dead hares they find so that they can be sent to the labs in Norwich for post-mortems. I don't think we are expected to post them. I am irritated enough by Post Office counter staff asking me, "What's in the parcel?" without having to say, "It's a dead hare, of course". No, email D.Bell@uea.ac.uk and I reckon the University of East Anglia biology department would arrange collection. This apparent virus mutation is particularly bad news for our iconic brown hares. Their numbers have declined by 80% in the last hundred years. Habitat loss including the removal of hedgerows, intensive farming, increased road traffic, shooting, and in some places illegal coursing with dogs, have all put pressure on our speedy and legendary hares. Br'er Rabbit will need all his wiles and survival tricks if this new virus takes hold.

Bridges

A footbridge over the Avon takes the path between two fishing lakes which were created by monks from the nearby Kenilworth Priory to provide the brethren with fresh fish, and it continues through the village of King's Newnham. To the left is Newnham Hall and standing by the river is a ruined tower. It's all that remains of the village church, most of which was pulled down in the sixteenth century after the place had been substantially abandoned. Why? Because the Duke of Northumberland, the extremely rich member of the aristocracy who owned huge tracts of land in the Midlands, had enclosed the common land, ruining many of the local farmers.

The next village along the Shakespeare Avon Way is Bretford, notable for a beautiful old bridge over the river with a series of low, curved arches. It's been repaired over the years in keeping with the original medieval construction. And on a modern bridge nearby, the Fosse Way crosses the Avon. This straight road is definitely of Roman origin, connecting Exeter in the south-west with Lincoln via Bath and Leicester. It may have started life as a defensive ditch against the Celts to the north-west. Fossa in Latin means ditch.

Our way takes us through the village of Wolston, where there's an impressive low viaduct spanning the river with nine arches. It was constructed in the 1830s by Robert Stephenson to carry the London to Birmingham Railway, Britain's first inter-city line. The viaduct is still in good nick and these days carries the West Coast Main Line. But Wolston's main claim to fame is below ground, in its geology.

The village gives its name to the Wolstonian Age of the geological history of the Earth, a part of the Pleistocene epoch. The Wolstonian Stage was literally ages ago, from 350,000 BC to 130,000 years BC. The Pleistocene period ended with the most recent ice age a mere 11,700 years ago, when sabre-toothed tigers were still around hunting giant elk. There's a skeleton of a Giant Irish Deer or Elk in the Warwickshire County Museum in Warwick. It was acquired by the museum in the 19th century after the bones were found well-preserved in an Irish peat bog.

After passing through Wolston, our track crosses The Centenary Way, a 98-mile footpath though Warwickshire created to celebrate the centenary of the County Council. Our waymarked path leads west to Ryton-on-Dunsmore while the river itself loops to the north through the Brandon Marsh Nature Reserve.

Brandon Marsh

It's a bit of a detour from the Shakespeare Way to Brandon Marsh, the headquarters of the Warwickshire Wildlife Trust, but it's certainly worth a visit at any time of the year. It is a superb reserve with woodland and a series of lakes fed by the meandering Avon, and is particularly valuable being so close to large conurbations. The city of Coventry is just four miles away to the north. There are large islands where terns, black-headed gulls and lapwings breed noisily. At this time of year the birds are in spanking fresh breeding plumage.

There are brightly coloured pochard with their chestnut heads, teal, shoveller with their heavy bills, black and white tufted ducks that dive for their food, and gadwall - mallard-sized ducks with finely patterned grey plumage and black patches under their tails. On the grassy banks beside one of the larger pools, there are hundreds of wigeon. These attractive ducks are feeding up ready for their long migration flight to their breeding grounds in Scandinavia, Iceland and Russia.

From the hides I can see a pair of avocets and a pure white little egret. Egrets are now fairly common here as the British breeding population moves up the country from the south coast – a result of our warming climate. And the much larger great white egret, normally seen across Asia, Africa and the Americas, is now a regular at Brandon. These changes in bird populations are happening incredibly quickly. In 1970 as few as 150 great egrets were recorded in the whole of Europe. By the turn of the 21st century they were appearing along Britain's south and east coasts. According to the Wildlife Trusts, in 2010 there were an estimated 1,000 great egrets seen in the UK, mainly in the south-east. In 2020 there were around 8,000 sighted all over England and Wales. As a result, in 2021, the Bird Guides magazine and website that monitors bird populations changed the status of the Great White Egret. It is no longer 'rare' in Britain. And that's official! But it's still a thrill to see one of these large egrets so close to busy roads and conurbations.

In the reed-beds, water rails are often heard squealing, otters are seen quite regularly, and sometimes a marsh harrier will appear, slowly quartering low over the waving reeds on wings held in a shallow v-shape. And on a cold, calm evening, there is always the chance of a spectacular murmuration.

Murmurations

On several occasions in early spring, I've joined a few other observers armed with their binoculars and cameras on a bank next to the reserve car park, overlooking a large reed bed, to see the starlings arrive at dusk. There are several suitable reed beds across the 220 acres of the reserve, and the starlings may choose any one of them. But the one next to the Visitor Centre seems to be favoured quite often. How the birds know where the roost will be each evening is anyone's guess. Maybe they communicate by Twitter. So fingers crossed that it is this reed bed tonight. The conditions are favourable. There is no wind and the sky is clear. With the sun an orange ball sinking slowly behind the trees to the left, and a full moon rising to the right, it is eerily quiet.

A robin perched on a fence breaks into song giving everyone a start. Then suddenly there is a small lozenge-shaped flock of starlings high over the reeds. Then more and more flocks join them until there is a large cloud of birds, separating and merging. But this is just the overture before the full performance. There's a hissing overhead, and looking up we can see two rivers of starlings, countless thousands of them coming in quite low over our heads, their wings making a noise like running water. Then they arc and plunge in amazing shapes, creating dark funnels and ripples, black against the pink-flushed sky – now a snake, now a whale.

This is a big starling roost. How many birds? It would be a wild guess, but other birdwatchers reckon at least 30,000 individuals have come together from across the midlands.

Many of the birds will be winter migrants that have flown across the North Sea from Scandinavia or Northern Russia to escape the severe cold there. They'll start to return at the end of March while our resident birds prepare to breed. And why do they flock together like this? Clearly there's safety in numbers. There are videos of peregrines swooping through murmurations, and finally giving up, empty-handed or empty-taloned. Even if the falcon gets lucky, the odds against being caught for each individual starling will be about thirty-thousand to one! And indeed, tonight, flying across below them in the dusk there is a sparrowhawk - a large female. She ignores them completely and disappears beyond the trees. She must know she hasn't a chance of picking off an individual bird in the whirling mass.

I think the main reason for these gathering is to keep warm on frosty nights. The birds huddle together, packed side by side along the reed stems. The RSPB suggests they also come together in a twittering crowd to exchange information, such as good feeding areas. As the light fades they are still arriving in huge numbers. By now the sky is darkened by the dense clouds of starlings wheeling and merging. And suddenly these avian clouds start to rain birds into the reed bed where they squeak and chatter. It's like dark liquid being poured out of a jug. Then in an instant, the show is over and the birds fall silent. The murmuration has been a truly memorable experience.

Firestorm and Tornado

After crossing open fields, Shakespeare's Avon Way rejoins the river bank and a short, surfaced path to the left leads to the Ryton Organic Gardens. It's a must-visit for any gardener, with 10 acres of vegetables, fruit and flowers, all managed entirely organically. You have to book in advance to join one of their garden tours when there are demonstrations by some of their expert gardeners. Last time I checked it costs a fiver to join a tour. The Ryton Gardens are also home to the Heritage Seed Library, conserving about 800 vegetable varieties that are not generally available. If you become a member you can get some packets of seed to try in your own veg patch or allotment.

Further along the path at Ryton-on-Dunsmore, an underpass gets us safely past the A45, the main road to Coventry. The city was infamously the first to be targeted by mass bombing raids in World War Two. On November 14th 1940, 520 German bombers dropped high explosives and incendiary bombs on Coventry in an operation codenamed 'Moonlight Sonata'. A firestorm engulfed the city centre, destroying the medieval cathedral. 4,300 homes were also destroyed and at least 560 people were killed. After the war, Coventry rose from the ashes with a splendid new cathedral and some modernist architecture, and recently it was chosen to be the UK's City of Culture.

Locals still talk of another destructive event, though by no means as devastating, and of natural origin. On a sunny day in April 1968, a suburb of Coventry, curiously called Barnacle, was hit by a freak weather event known as The Coventry Tornado. According to the Coventry Evening Telegraph, buildings and caravans were wrecked, trees were uprooted and the residents of Barnacle had to cling on tight. Terry Skelhorn said, "It was a nice day with blue skies. I looked across at this great big Mr. Whippy cone coming over. It picked up 20 cows from the field over at Brindley's Farm and you could see the cows going round and round!" Marlene and Chris Whitehead told reporters, "We'd just got into the house when it went dark and the windows all came in. We thought a plane had crashed." A flock of chickens was carried off and they were found later in neighbouring Bullington - apparently unharmed apart from some ruffled feathers.

After Ryton-on-Dunsmore, the path goes through the grounds of the now abandoned Peugeot car factory. This has a significant place in the history of the British motor industry. Built just before WW2, the factory produced aircraft engines during the war, then the Rootes Group took it over to produce cars with names only the older generations will recognise: Sunbeam, Hillman, Singer and Humber, before the Americans kindly came in with the Chrysler marque to take over a failing company, followed by the French car-maker, Peugeot. Our path takes us past huge empty car parks that used to have rows of gleaming new Hillman Hunters and Singer Gazelles.

Suddenly it's Spring

As we approach Bubbenhall across open fields and then along some minor roads, it would be a crime to miss the Ryton Pools, especially as the weather towards the end of March has turned extremely mild with a southerly airstream and bright sunshine. By the end of the month the temperature in the Midlands has reached 22 degrees celsius. It's even warmer to the south-east with 29 degrees recorded, making it the hottest March day in Britain for 53 years. The trees by the river are glowing lemon yellow in the sunshine, with soft oval catkins on the pussy willow – traditionally an Easter decoration for your home - and the taller weeping willows cloaked in curly catkins of yellow and pale green.

A short lane to the left of the Avon Way takes us to the visitor centre with a cafe and information boards about the wildlife seen there recently. Ryton Pools Country Park is run by the County Council, with the adjoining Bubbenhall Wood under the care of the Warwickshire Wildlife Trust. This is a valuable patch of ancient woodland. It's mentioned in the Domesday Book of 1086, listed as 2 furlongs long and two furlongs wide; that's about the size of a dozen football pitches. The Ryton Pools area is beautifully managed, with paved or asphalt paths all around the 100 acre site and hides and viewing screens at the chain of pools. It's full-on Spring. The summer migrants are pouring into the country from the Mediterranean and sub-Saharan Africa and immediately begin searching for a mate. From the oak trees beside the main stream feeding the Avon, I can hear chiffchaffs calling their name, the trickling cascading song of the willow warbler, and the fruitier song of the blackcap.

Overhead there are two twittering swallows, the first of the year for me, brought by the southerly winds. They a sure sign that spring has arrived and always a joy to see. And then they are joined by a large group of sand martins swooping low overhead. Often the first to arrive here from Africa, they are a particular favourite of mine with their cheery chirrup. They are pale brown with white chests and a brown collar, and they are very agile in flight, twisting and turning as they hawk for flying insects, often in small groups.

From the hide overlooking the main pool there's also plenty of action to watch. The coots are squabbling over territory, sitting back in the water and scrabbling at each other with their enormous feet while squawking angrily. Two little grebes are also making a bit of a racket, with their sharp trilling call, rather like a hysterical giggle. And there's a sudden flash of electric blue low over the water, like a bolt from a crossbow, and the kingfisher obligingly alights on a fence post less than 50 feet from the hide. It's a female, identified by the orange lower mandible of her bill. The male has an all black bill. For such a brightly coloured bird, the kingfisher is quite difficult to spot because it is small – at 16 cm from beak-tip to tail it's not much bigger than a sparrow. And it flies fast and straight – easy to miss. So it is great to see this individual in full sunlight with its bright orange chest, blue-green back and a metallic pale blue rump that flashes as it flies off. And there she goes, emitting the characteristic single loud 'peep' as she shoots away over the tangled fringe of the pool.

And then I witness a deadly drama. A mallard duck has six small ducklings dabbling about near the reeds. One is further out towards the centre of the pool. Suddenly there is a swoosh and a splash, the ripples subside, and the duckling has gone. Almost certainly it had been taken by a pike right in front of the hide. Mallard have large broods. I've seen a family of 14 newly-hatched ducklings on the Avon, and the mother duck must try to keep them as close to her as she can to deter crows, gulls and other predators. But there isn't much she can do to defend against the pike! She'll be fortunate if two or three of her ducklings survive the spring.

At any time of year the Ryton Pools are worth a visit. There are dragonflies aplenty in the summer, a variety of meadow flowers, and all sorts of fungi in the autumn. Walking back to the Avon Way in this unusually warm March weather, there are small tortoiseshell and lemon-yellow brimstone butterflies fluttering in the grass beside the path. These individuals will have hibernated through the winter. Other butterflies will emerge from their pupae in May and June and will be joined by some species, such as the painted lady, that migrate from mainland Europe across the Channel, sometimes in huge numbers. Creamy-white blackthorn blossom is beginning to adorn the hedgerows. Spring has certainly arrived early.

April

Bubbenhall to Guy's Cliffe

It was a lover and his lass,
With a hey, and a ho, and a hey nonino,
That o'er the green corn-field did pass,
In the spring time, the only pretty ring time,
When birds do sing, hey ding a ding, ding;
Sweet lovers love the spring.
(As You Like It. Act V Scene 3)

Treecreeper

Slow trails and fast trains

Our route westward now passes through the attractive village of Bubbenhall, with its whitewashed Malt Shovel Inn, and the Shakespeare Avon Way then leaves the river awhile, inclining south and following public footpaths and minor roads until it rejoins the Avon at Leamington Spa. But I'm staying closer to the course of the river by continuing westward along Stareton Lane to visit the Stoneleigh Abbey Estate with its connections to Jane Austen's family, and also with plenty of wildlife undisturbed by traffic.

The Avon cuts through the Stoneleigh Park Golf Course where the river is a hazard on the 18th hole, called, unsurprisingly, The Avon Hole. I wonder how many golf balls have nestled into the sandy bottom of the river here, and how many expletives have been heard as they did so. The River Sowe joins the Avon here from the north, swelling the waters as it loops round to Stoneleigh Abbey. It's worth stopping to look at Stare Bridge spanning the Avon near Stareton.

This is a packhorse bridge dating from late medieval times, and may have been built by the monks at Stoneleigh Abbey. It's a beautiful low bridge made of the local red sandstone – only 10 feet wide but nearly 100 yards long, with nine arches, carrying the old road on a raised causeway across the Avon flood plain. As the name suggests, packhorse bridges were not designed for carts, but for horses and mules loaded with various goods. The parapets of the Stare Bridge were kept low so that the horses' panniers would be clear of the sides. Standing on this lovely old bridge one can almost feel part of history.

But just a few hundred yards away it is far from a timeless, peaceful scene. There is a constant throb of heavy machinery. Bulldozers and gigantic tip-up trucks are overshadowed by diggers with toothed mouths, like dinosaurs, gouging gobbets out of the sandy Warwickshire earth. For we have come across the route of the HS2 high-speed line from London to Birmingham; at time of writing it is tearing its way through the Midlands. This Phase One was estimated to cost £55 billion. The latest estimate I've seen puts it at up to £98 billion, but that was at 2019 prices before high inflation began to bite. And it was before the Leeds leg was cancelled. So goodness knows what the final bill might be. A former executive said that the initial estimate for buying land and property was "enormously wrong". Buying-up property on this section alone has cost £5 billion, five times the estimate.

The HS2 route goes straight through Stoneleigh Park. This is not to be confused with the deer park of Stoneleigh Abbey next door. Stoneleigh Park is owned by the Royal Agricultural Society of England and is a science park, with 60 or so companies and organisations related to innovative farming, and rural businesses. As it heads for the new Curzon Street Station in Birmingham, the high speed line will cross the Avon here on a viaduct, somewhat wider and higher than the 15th century packhorse bridge. It might be quite impressive. I wonder if it will still be standing in 550 years time, and if so, whether people will love its old-world charm and muse about the times when people travelled about on trains.

Stoneleigh Abbey and Jane Austen's mother

A little to the south of the HS2 route are the grounds of Stoneleigh Abbey, now converted into splendid apartments. At time of writing it will cost you seven quid to wander through the estate; but to my mind it is well worth this contribution to its upkeep. The house and estate are very attractive with an interesting history. In 1154, Henry II granted this land to a group of Cistercian monks. But 400 years later, when another Henry was dissolving the monasteries and seizing their wealth, the estate was acquired by a supporter of the monarchy, the Lord Mayor of London no less, one Sir Thomas Leigh. The Leigh family became the largest landowner in Warwickshire, and the abbey was turned into a stately home. In the eighteenth century, it was extended with an impressive four-storey west wing designed by Francis Smith in his favoured English Baroque style. We will find out more about 'Smith of Warwick' when we reach the county town.

There's a strong connection with Jane Austen here at Stoneleigh. Her mother, born Cassandra Leigh, was a distant relative of Sir Thomas Leigh of Stoneleigh. Recently widowed, Mrs. Austen and her two daughters were staying with her cousin, another Thomas - the Reverend Thomas Leigh of Adlestrop, Gloucestershire - when news arrived of the death of Mary Leigh the owner of Stoneleigh. She had no children. Who would inherit? Apparently the Austens and Leighs piled into carriages and immediately sped to the Stoneleigh estate for Rev. Thomas to claim his inheritance. Mrs. Austen, Jane and her sister Cassandra, stayed at Stoneleigh for ten days and were clearly bowled over by its size and elegance. Mrs. Austen's long and ecstatic letters to her daughter-in-law have survived to give us a picture of the visit to Stoneleigh.

"I had no idea of it being so beautiful. The Avon runs near the house amid green meadows, bounded by large and beautiful woods, full of delightful walks". The recent death of Mrs. Austen's husband, Jane's father, had left the family insecure financially. It must have been reassuring that their cousin Thomas had come into a fortune. Jane never revisited Stoneleigh Abbey, but it pops up in different guises in her famous novels. In 'Mansfield Park' the descriptions of the fictitious Sotherton Court sound like a description of

Stoneleigh, including the grounds, the chapel and the nearby village with almshouses. 'Northanger Abbey' is set in an old abbey converted into a country home.

One of the largest English oaks in the country stands in the grounds. With a girth of 9.2 metres it is estimated to be around a thousand years old. Even in Shakespeare's lifetime this would have been a very old tree. The grounds at Stoneleigh were laid out by Humphrey Repton, who was at the time as much in demand as Capability Brown for devising the 'natural' or pastoral look, with vistas that were unlike the regimented formal gardens of earlier stately homes and palaces. Repton used sluices to divert part of the Avon so that it would meander prettily across the front of the big house, with a picturesque bridge, and a 'mirror lake' to reflect the grand frontage of the house. And for me the languid river and lake work beautifully. From the terrace I can see the grey heron stalking the reedy fringe of the river; there are the mallard and tufted ducks in full breeding plumage, and on a sandy island there are seven pale ducks with chestnut-brown heads, resting by the water's edge.

Different bills

These are goosander, the largest of the family of sawbill ducks. The family name relates to the sharp jagged edges of their narrow beaks. These ducks don't dabble for weeds; they dive and catch fish, and the 'sawbills' mean they can cling on to their wriggling prey. There are two other species of sawbill ducks that can be seen in Britain; the smaller red-breasted merganser that favours upland streams, and the smew, a winter visitor from the north, with the male exotically plumed in white and black. Smew are unlikely to be seen in the middle of England, unless on a large reservoir. The smew's cousin the goosander is more likely on inland rivers but is far from common; so it is great to see a family party quite close in the Stoneleigh Abbey grounds.

And what's this? An unmistakeable trilling and piping says there are oystercatchers about. Yes, there they are - a pair standing on the railings right in front of the big house, strikingly black and white with long, bright red bills that are strong and flattened to enable them to prise open cockles and mussels, their main diet on the coast. I think opening an oyster might be too much of a challenge even with that powerful bill. The call of the oystercatcher is the sound of summer holidays by the coast, but some nest inland and feed on worms in open fields. For some reason the collective noun for a group of oystercatchers is a 'parcel'. Or sometimes it's a 'stew' of oystercatchers! I don't much like the idea of oystercatcher stew; it might taste a bit fishy. But it's good to find these striking birds just two miles from the large town of Kenilworth, and their loud piping is always uplifting. The oystercatcher is bird number 80 on my list for this year along the Warwickshire Avon. Will it be possible to get to 100? Perhaps not. We will see.

To the east of the Avon, the Shakespeare Way drives south through Weston-under-Wetherley. A wetherley is a castrated ram, so there would have been a meadow nearby where these lambs were fattened up ready to be chopped into chops. The village of Weston has an impressive church dedicated to St. Michael, but not much else of note, apart from the fact that in November 1605 a group of men on horseback dashed clattering through the village, whipping their mounts desperately. Among them was Robert Catesby, the leader of The Gunpowder Plot, who with his fellow conspirators was fleeing London after the arrest of Guy Fawkes, with the king's men in hot pursuit. Apparently they were on their way to

Wales, via Warwick Castle where they stole fresh horses. Their flight was in vain. Cornered at Holbeche House in what is now Dudley in the West Midlands, Catesby was shot dead. That wasn't enough for the king's supporters. After burial, Catesby's body was exhumed and beheaded, and the head of the traitor was displayed outside Parliament House – just to dissuade anyone one else from thinking of blowing the king to kingdom come.

I've continued to take footpaths and minor roads to stay closer to the river. It would be a great shame to miss Guy's Cliffe with its gothic ruins and legends of love and sacrifice. Just to the south of Stoneleigh Park is a pretty village that sounds like a sneeze. Ashow has no more than 50 houses and cottages, many of them half-timbered with the characteristic orange brick of this area. The Church of the Assumption of Our Lady, dating back to the early 12th century, stands hard by the rippling waters of the Avon. It's a tranquil spot. There's an old footbridge over the Avon heading across the fields to the south. The bridge is very narrow with hand rails tilting out, perhaps to allow you carry your picnic basket.

I can hear a very soft 'sip sip' from an oak tree beside the track. And there walking up the trunk at about head height, undisturbed by my presence, is a treecreeper. What an amazing beak – a very thin curved bill, like a surgical instrument. It levers off flakes of bark that flutter down at my feet as it seeks insects, spiders and woodlice hiding underneath. You would think this delicate bill would snap. It must be made of very tough stuff. Birds' bills are interesting. They are one of the key features that define a creature as a bird. It has a beak! And birds use them for just about everything - to collect food, preen, fight, court, (such as pigeons billing and cooing), chop holes in trees, weave nests, and more. But for a bird to fly, this strong bill must weigh as little as possible.

Beaks are covered with a sheath of a tough but quite lightweight material called keratin, which grows continuously because a beak wears down with use. The strength of the bill, even for a little treecreeper, comes from two boney projections from the skull – the upper and lower mandibles. To be technical, they are covered with a thin keratinised layer of epidermis known as the rhamphotheca. In most species, two holes known as nares lead to the respiratory system. These are the breathing holes, and also, as with humans, they carry scent organs.

Can birds smell?

For a very long time it has been widely thought by biologists that birds have a poor sense of smell and taste. After all, in the lab it was established in the early nineteen hundreds that birds have up to 500 tastebuds, whereas humans have up to 10,000! But recent research shows that the avian sense of smell and taste depends on the species and their food-hunting needs. It's important for birds to be able to identify bitterness, to avoid ingesting dietary toxins, but only a small number of species such as parrots and hummingbirds seem to have the ability to identify sweetness as we humans do.

For example, a shearwater which spends most of its life cruising low over the sea picking off bits of dead marine life has a pretty good sense of smell. And vultures wheeling high over a forest canopy can home-in on a rotting carcase from a couple of miles away. In a Spanish study of blue tits, researchers painted weasel scent around the entrances of a number of nest boxes. (Don't ask me how they got hold of a pot of weasel scent). The blue tits that had been hopping in and out to feed their broods hesitated, and had to pluck up courage to go in. The researchers concluded that the birds smelled the weasel musk and feared that their chief predator might be inside the box.

And surely some birds can detect pheromones? In the spring, water fowl are driven sex-mad by pheromones. So what are they? Hormones work inside your body and may affect your mood or general state of health. Pheromones are secreted outside your body and may affect others in various ways. These mysterious secretions are massively important in the insect world, particularly in the search for mating partners. And the mallard drakes relentlessly pursuing females are being drawn by the alluring pheromones. There is a continuing scientific debate about whether humans are influenced by pheromones in a similar way. Napoleon famously sent word ahead to Josephine saying, "Ne te lave pas, j'accours et dans huit jours je suis là". (Don't wash. I'm coming and in eight days will be there'), suggesting he was turned on by her smell. Or maybe the story is just British propaganda to suggest he was a crude peasant.

It's interesting that there is a multi-billion dollar global business selling very expensive products that promise sexual conquests if you cream them on, dab them on, bathe in them, stick them under your arms or behind your ears. But though scientific research suggests that mammals can detect pheromones through an organ in the nose called the vomeronasal (VNO), otherwise known as Jacobson's Organ, it seems that the VNO in humans atrophies after birth and then consists of useless pits. So detecting pheromones isn't quite the same as using your sense of smell. It seems we humans probably can't pick up pheromone signals from the opposite sex. Then again – do scientists know everything?

Mills

Our route to Leamington goes through another attractive hamlet, Blackdown, notable for its old mill with a tall brick chimney. County records show there has been a mill here since medieval times. It was in use until the 1920s and the waterwheel is still in position. There were dozens of mills dotted along the Avon in times gone by. Water power was vital for milling grain from the surrounding farms and in some cases in later years produced electricity for the big manor houses of the landowners. The flowing water controlled by sluices was an entirely reliable energy source, unlike the wind. Millers using windmills could be becalmed for days. Modern windmills have a similar problem in periods of calm weather.

The next hamlet on our route is Old Milverton, with its parish church of St. James standing on a ridge in open countryside. In the churchyard is the grave of Sir George Catlin, the husband of Vera Brittan, famed pacifist, feminist, and author of the 'Testament of Youth'. In fact a bit of Vera is also here. Her ashes were divided to be beside the graves of her husband and her brother who died in Italy in WW1. There is a long straight path down a sloping field sown with a mixture of wheat and rye. To my left, a small bird not much bigger than a blackbird is dashing low across the ground scattering the meadow pipits and chaffinches. It twists and turns but fails to make a kill, and disappears over the ridge at high speed. It was a merlin, probably a female judging by its size. The male is smaller. What a treat to see this dynamic little falcon, our smallest bird of prey, even briefly. Merlins are endangered but seem to be recovering from a population crash in the 20th century, with more sightings in the midlands, particularly in the winter and spring.

The path leads through a kissing gate to a footbridge across the river and an old cobbled path to The Saxon Mill. This is a splendid gastro pub in a converted mill of some antiquity - the wheel is incorporated in the dining area - and just outside is a rushing weir. It is a delightful spot, particularly on warm summer days when you can dine outside overlooking this branch of the Avon with its weeping willows kissing the surface of the water, and young trout gathering above the weir hoping for a breadcrumb or two.

Just a short distance along the path beside the river, there is a wonderful romantic ruin on the far bank, perched on an outcrop of russet Warwickshire sandstone with a drop of forty feet to the Avon and penetrated by a series of caves. This is Guy's Cliffe House, steeped in legend.

Guy of Warwick

This rocky bluff by the Avon is named after Guy of Warwick. You may not have heard of this hero, but in parts of France, Germany, and Austria he is almost as well known as Robin Hood. 'Gui de Warewic' in Romance literature is a model of chivalric behaviour - brave, honourable, loyal and devout. He is honoured in countless medieval and 17th century poems, plays, songs and tales of derring-do. In the legend, the yeoman Guy falls in love with the lady Felice, (meaning Happiness), the daughter of the Earl of Warwick. To prove his worthiness and to become a knight, he sets off on a journey slaying dragons, giants and monsters, starting with the Dun Cow, the huge beast causing trouble around Dunsmore Heath. He then defeated the Viking champion, the giant Colbrand, at Winchester, and continued to rid communities of terrible beasts across Europe as far as Constantinople. Guy of Warwick and Colbrand the Giant are mentioned in Shakespeare's Henry VIII. A servant who failed to prevent a drunken mob raiding the palace larder, says he couldn't stop them. "I am not Samson, nor Sir Guy, nor Colbrand to mow 'em down before me".

To cut a long story short, and it is a very long legend, Guy returns home, is knighted, and wins the heart of the girl.

But they do not live happy ever after. Guy is gripped by conscience. He shouldn't have been so violent and soaked in blood. God speaks to him and he sets off on a pilgrimage to the Holy Land to purge his sins. Perhaps Felice was left doing embroidery in what is now called 'Guy's Tower', in Warwick Castle.

Guy returns, but for reasons that are not entirely clear, he doesn't make himself known to his beloved wife, but lives as a religious hermit in a cave in the sandstone cliff overlooking the Avon. Only when he is at death's door does he send for Felice. She rushes to his side and he dies in her arms. Did Guy really exist? Historians note that the 11th century Sheriff of Warwickshire shortly before the Norman conquest, had a daughter with the unusual name of Felicia.

Guy's Cliffe House

As for Guy's Cliffe House, named after the legend of our local hero, it has a pretty extraordinary history itself. First, there was a chantry in the cliff, commissioned by Henry V who was later portrayed so heroically by Shakespeare. It was established in 1423, shortly after Henry's death, on the supposed site of Guy of Warwick's hermitage. It was called the Chapel of St. Mary Magdalene. The stables and storerooms carved into the rock remain to this day. The great house on top of the cliff was started in the mid-eighteenth century by a slightly less heroic figure, a rich merchant called Samuel Greatheed who was the Member of Parliament for Coventry. He owned sugar plantations in the West Indies and no fewer than 230 slaves. On his death the estates in England and the West Indies were inherited by his son, Bertie, who was an enlightened man of many talents. He was a supporter of the abolition of slavery and described the sugar plantation as his "odious property".

Nevertheless he continued to benefit from the significant income from trading in sugar and slaves, travelling across Europe with his wife, Ann, who was also his first cousin, and with his son, also called Bertie. They lived for a while in Germany and France where he was recognised as a talented writer and artist. His painting skill came in handy when they were held as prisoners of war in Paris in 1803. His portrait of Napoleon impressed the Emperor, and Bertie and his family were allowed to leave for Italy. The following year, in Vicenza, his son contracted flu and died, leaving Bertie without an heir. But then it emerged that he had been having a secret affair with a woman in Dresden and had an illegitimate daughter called Ann Caroline. The girl was brought to England and raised at Guy's Cliffe. She went on to marry Lord Charles Greatheed Bertie Percy, the son of Algernon Percy, the Earl of Beverley. Algernon's older brother, George, was the immensely wealthy Duke of Northumberland. So Ann did alright for herself.

Bertie meanwhile was investing his wealth in the development of the new Georgian spa town at Leamington Priors, which later became known as Leamington Spa. He bought up building plots on the west side of what is now the Parade in Leamington, and after the rather fortunate discovery of a salty spring on his land, became a partner in the construction of the Royal Pump Rooms on the site. I wonder how many residents of elegant Leamington are aware that it was founded on the trade in sugar, rum and slaves.

A Romantic Ruin

Guy's Cliffe House was used as a hospital in World War I, and in World War II became a school for evacuated children. After the war the estate was sold and the house fell into disrepair.

By 1966 the roof had fallen in and it had become a popular location for films. In 1992, during the filming for Granada TV of 'The Adventures of Sherlock Homes – The Last Vampyre', with Jeremy Brett as the inscrutable sleuth, a scene with a fire got out of control and badly damaged the building. Now the spectacular ruin is used by the Freemasons - of course I can't tell you what they do in there, but I'm told the masonic rooms are very splendid - and the ruin is maintained by The Friends of Guy's Cliffe. Across the Coventry Road the old kitchen garden surrounded by high brick walls has been beautifully restored by volunteers. Guy's Cliffe Walled Garden is regularly open to the public and is well worth a visit.

You can book guided tours of the ruined house on some days in the year, and for those interested in paranormal activities there are occasional ghost hunts staged overnight, run by a company called 'Haunted Happenings'. The ruin is also occupied by flocks of jackdaws, feral pigeons and stock doves, and sometimes the hooting of the tawny owl completes the gothic atmosphere.

May

Leamington Spa to Warwick

Love, whose month is ever May,
Spied a blossom passing fair
Playing in the wanton air.
(Love's Labour's Lost. Act IV Scene 3)

House Martin

Royal Boom Town

In Love's Labour's Lost, the love-struck Dumaine compares the out-of-reach girl with a blossom blown past by the wind. And yes, this stretch of Shakespeare's Avon Way passes a leisure facility called Newbold Comyn Park where pink and white cherry blossom is scattering in the breeze. There's a golf course and an indoor swimming pool, then suddenly the path is alongside the River Leam, pronounced "Lem", just to the east of Leamington, named after its river.

Apologies - that should be just to the east of 'Royal Leamington Spa' to give this town its full regal title. Some of the locals like to keep the Spa bit if not the Royal bit. That was added graciously by Queen Victoria in 1838; she was a big fan of the health properties of salty water, and her patronage helped the place to boom. She had visited the town as a princess in 1830 and returned as Queen in 1858. There is a splendid statue of Victoria at the bottom of the main street, The Parade. Is she focussing her unamused gaze on a bar on the other side of the road? She probably thinks you should be drinking Leamington Spa water instead. In fact you can still do this today, outside the Royal Pump Rooms in Bath Street. I leave it to you to decide which you prefer - a glass of bitter mineral water, or a foaming pint of bitter.

Originally no more than a smallholding by the river, called in Anglo-Saxon, 'Lemen-tun', meaning the farm by the Leam, the place gets a mention in the Domesday book as 'Lemintone' and became known as 'Leamington Priors'. It remained as a pretty insignificant hamlet near the market town of Warwick until 1784, when William Abbotts and Benjamin Satchwell discovered a saline spring near the parish church. They drilled half a dozen wells nearby and they all came up with the right mineral content. Bingo!

With the financial backing of Bertie Greatheed of Guy's Cliffe, they began developing the area to the north of the river Leam with smart hotels, bath houses and pump rooms, where guests could take the rather foul-tasting waters. The moneyed classes living in smokey London and Birmingham were suddenly crazy for health spas, and Leamington experienced the most rapid expansion of any town in England. The population recorded in the national census of 1801 was just 315. Fifty years later it had grown to nearly sixteen thousand.

The opening of a railway station on the main line between London and Birmingham in 1852 gave the place a huge boost. By 1901 the population was nearly twenty-seven thousand, without counting the visitors. The investors could hardly keep up, building assembly rooms, hot and cold baths, hotels, municipal buildings and smart residential streets as fast as they could. The architecture of Leamington is a combination of Georgian and Victorian, with elegant crescents and wide avenues.

The developers were enlightened enough to see that the riverbanks should not be built upon, and were perfect for healthy walking and contact with nature. So the Leam, heading for its junction with the Avon, passes through the delightful Jephson Gardens in the centre of Leamington, with pathways, flowerbeds, pools, a glasshouse with exotic plants, and artwork demonstrating Leamington's recent reputation as a centre for the creative arts. Jephson Gardens and the Mill Gardens on the opposite bank are part of The Spa Gardens, a ribbon of riverside parks in Leamington that are listed as Grade II on the English Heritage register of historic parks and gardens. The local council protects them fiercely. No cycling and no fishing in Jephson Gardens. Dogs must be kept on leads. The wildlife seems to appreciate this protection. Wildfowl abound on a small lake in the park, with flotillas of brown and yellow peeping ducklings, the flower beds are alive with butterflies, and the trees and shrubs are filled with April birdsong.

New Residents

Overhead there's a sharp, metallic squeaking, and looking up, I can see a peregrine falcon heading towards the Town Hall with its fast wingbeat. Judging by its size this is the male or tiercel, so called because it is about a third smaller than the female. A pair moved in to the centre of town a few years ago and the District Council made them welcome. With the help of Warwickshire Wildlife Trust, they placed a shallow tray of gravel in the top part of the Town Hall clock tower and the birds duly adopted it as their nest site, or 'scrape', successfully rearing young each year.

This year the peregrines took it in turns to incubate four rich-brown eggs, and all have hatched. Anyone with a computer can watch the white fluffy chicks, live, in close-up and full colour, thanks to webcams in the tower. Both parents have bright yellow 'ceres' at the base of their hooked bill – a sign that they are healthy birds. They need plenty of nourishment to produce the yellow pigment. After the chicks hatch it becomes rather a gruesome show as the parents bring in carcasses of pigeons, starlings and occasionally gulls and other prey, and tenderly feed their offspring with gobbets of flesh.

Sometimes the last chick to hatch is bullied by the others and doesn't survive. But these four young peregrines are all growing fast on this protein-rich diet, and when they fledge, the people of Leamington will be treated to some fabulous aerial displays as the young birds learn their important flying skills, and are shown how to hunt by their parents, sometimes directly above Jephson Gardens in the centre of town.

Ahead of his Time?

So who was Jephson, named in these lovely gardens and a with a domed classical-style shrine to his memory amongst the shrubbery? It seems he was a combination of what you know and who you know. A well-qualified 'surgeon apothecary' and Doctor of Medicine, he had connections with many influential members of society, and he brought them to Leamington Spa. He and his wife regularly entertained a hundred or more people to dances and suppers in the mansion he had built in Warwick Street. 'Beech Lawn' was a substantial twenty-room house standing in three acres of garden with half-a-dozen resident staff. Dr. Jephson was earning the equivalent of £1.5 million a year at today's values. That said, two hours of each morning were set aside for treating the poor and any fee which he earned on a Sunday was distributed among his poor patients, which is a generous touch don't you think?

And it is why the blue plaque attached to his former house at 118 The Parade reads: 'Dr. Henry Jephson – physician and philanthropist'. And writing his obituary, his lifelong friend and fellow physician Dr Thomas Thursfield had this to say about Henry Jephson: "In twenty years he had what was probably, and possibly still is, the most extraordinary success ever achieved by any physician. Henry Jephson was a man ahead of his time." His treatment of many of his patients included drinking (Leamington Spa) water, eating fresh vegetables, and lots of walking. The benefits of a healthy diet including lots of fresh veg, and regular exercise are now widely advocated as the key to a healthier and quite possible a longer life.

And here are a couple of little known facts about Leamington. It had a big part to play in the founding of lawn tennis as an international sport. The first lawn tennis club in the world was set up here by a couple of enthusiasts for the new outdoor version of real tennis, and the rules were drawn up in 1874 at Leamington Tennis Club, just behind the Manor House Hotel. They have been followed largely unaltered to this day. It was three years later that a croquet club in Wimbledon decided to include lawn tennis. Fifteen-love to Leamington I reckon. The town still has an indoor real tennis court at its Leamington Tennis Court Club. Founded in 1846, it's the oldest Real Tennis Club in the world.

Leamington has now gone high-tech, as a major centre of the gaming industry, with a cluster of 32 studios employing 2,000 highly-skilled people creating computer games. The town has acquired a new nickname – 'Silicon Spa'. It happened thanks to the vision of two young men, the Darling brothers, who started up a business back in the 1980s that would ultimately be called Codemasters. They chose to base themselves in Leamington because, they said, it had lots of bars and a great nightlife. From that silicon spring, rather than a saline spring, gushed Silicon Spa, with other software developers being attracted to the area. The acquisition of Codemasters by the big Electronic Arts company in 2021 cost £1 billion.

Leamington is also the location of a new so-called mega-lab designed to identify, test and trace virus samples during pandemics such as Covid-19. Opened in August 2021 it was designed to process thousands of Covid-19 samples per day. But almost immediately afterwards, with the infection rate at an all-time high, the government decided to abandon its much-criticised test and trace programme. The lab that was designed to employ hundreds of scientists had been warmly welcomed in high-tech Leamington, but it finished up working at less than a fifth of its intended capacity and an independent investigation concluding that the lab had cost nearly double its allocated budget. Let's hope it won't be needed to tackle another pandemic in the foreseeable future.

Otters return

The River Leam joins the Avon between Leamington and Warwick. Despite being surrounded by housing, retail developments, schools and business parks, it is worth keeping your eyes peeled for otters here. I think along this stretch of the Leam there may be a family holed up, or should that be holted up? They are seen sometimes, and two otter cubs or 'kits' have been filmed playing in the middle of the river just below a footbridge in the Jephson Gardens. The return of otters to the Avon and its tributaries has happened recently and quickly, and they benefitted from some helping hands.

The Warwickshire Wildlife Trust led the way in trying to encourage otters back to midland rivers. In the 1990s these charismatic animals were never seen in the heart of England. With no otters about, mink had taken over the river banks, devastating the water vole population and predating ground nesting birds. The only otters I'd ever seen were in northern Scotland, at some distance through binoculars. The Trust's Otter Task Force of about 20 volunteers with the support of the Environment Agency built a complex system of more than 30 otter holts at secret locations along the banks of rivers such as the Avon.

It worked, and aided by mink-trapping and improved water quality in the Avon, the otters are returning in increasing numbers. Pete Sanders, a Biodiversity Officer at the Wildlife Trust, has been studying otters in the Midlands for 25 years. He says, "We can say with pride that these incredible creatures are back on every river in Warwickshire, and populations are rising". They are semi-nocturnal, largely active at night, but there is still the chance of seeing an otter in the Warwickshire Avon in broad daylight. I have seen them on several occasions in the section of the river between Leamington and Warwick, including very close views right in the centre of Warwick. I think otters are starting to learn to live with humans.

The County Town

Warwick with its famous fortress is my home town, so I know this stretch of the Avon very well. The Shakespeare Way arrives in the historic county town via St. Nicholas Park. As an urban park it's got everything. Originally a meadow, it was laid out in the 1930s with formal gardens and a children's playground. After the Second World War, it was extended to the east with tennis courts, playing fields, and an open-air swimming pool beside the river. Later, a small children's funfair was added, along with a large leisure centre with a heated indoor pool replacing the chillier outdoor one fed by the Avon. That was filled-in; trees were planted, and it has tuned into a mature copse. There are now 80 different species of tree in St. Nicholas Park.

The interesting area for naturalists is up river from the formal section and play areas. The Kingfisher Pools on the south side of the Avon have reed beds, tangles of scrub, some lines of mature trees, and an adjoining area of privately-owned rough fields. For a park surrounded by busy roads and houses, it is a remarkable haven for wildlife, particularly in May when the migrant warblers are at full throttle declaring their territory. Willow warblers can be heard all along this stretch of the river, producing their delicate downward cascading song. Chiffchaffs, that look almost identical to willow warblers, can be identified easily by their 'chiff-chaff' call. In fact in the eighteenth century, naturalists thought the willow warbler, chiffchaff and wood warbler were all the same bird – the 'willow wren'. It was the keenly observant vicar of Selborne, Gilbert White, who worked out from their songs they must be different species.

Standing by the pools I can hear two sedge warblers pouring out their varied song, squeaking, trilling and chattering. There's one, clinging to a reed stem. It is a very attractive little warbler with a prominent creamy supercilium over its eye and a dark crown, giving it an unmistakable stripy-headed look. The song of the reed warbler can be confused with the sedge warbler, but it is more monotonous and scratchy, and the reed warbler tends to stay hidden. If you do spot one, they are plain brown with a pale underside; no stripy head.

Much more visible are the whitethroats. They chatter at you crossly from the brambles, have a short scratchy song, and occasionally rise almost vertically in their display flight, parachuting down to a prominent perch before diving back into the undergrowth. And from a patch of brambles on the river bank I can hear another warbler, the lesser whitethroat, which has a very different song from its namesake, the common whitethroat. It's a low-key chatter followed immediately by a loud and pure trill that carries for hundreds of yards.

From a tangle of reeds by the water's edge I can hear a strange squealing and know it is the very elusive water rail. I wait and watch for a full twenty minutes, and eventually a curved red bill appears. I stay motionless but to no avail; goodbye rail. It has spotted this dangerous human and bobbed back into the tangled cover.

The paved path beside the river in St. Nicholas' Park is attractively overhung by weeping willows with pale yellow fronds of young leaves flickering in the breeze. In fact the riverside in May is a symphony of yellows, with clumps of marsh marigolds glowing like polished metal in the sun, stands of yellow iris by the pools, meadow buttercups mingling as high as an elephant's eye with cow parsley and escaped oilseed rape along the riverbanks.

Directly ahead is an elegant single-arch bridge over the river carrying the road to Banbury. 'Castle Bridge' was built by the 2nd Earl of Warwick , George Greville, in 1793. It required a special Act of Parliament to agree the deal by which the Earl would pay for a new, wider bridge to replace the old and unsafe bridge over the Avon at the weir below the castle, on condition that the Earl could take the lands between the castle and the new bridge and road. The deal was done. The bridge and new road from the south cost £3,258; probably small change for the immensely wealthy Earl of Warwick. The new road bridge was opened in the nick of time. Two years later, the medieval bridge, built in about the year 1200, was swept away in a flood.

The Mighty Castle

Beyond the Castle Bridge and the remains of the old bridge is the vertical curtain wall of Warwick Castle, one of the biggest and most impressive Norman fortresses in Europe. The view of the castle from the bridge has been painted many times, including by the Venetian artist Canaletto, and more recently it's been photographed many times more. A selfie on Castle Bridge is a must for any visitor to Warwick, especially as the mighty castle is curiously hidden behind trees when you are in the town.

Less than two years after his victory over the Anglo-Saxons at Hastings in 1066, William the Conqueror began building a castle here, (then a wooden motte and bailey). It was a key location. Its garrison would suppress any rebellions in the Midlands and the Welsh borders. Warwick Castle was built on a sandstone cliff on a bend in the Avon, the site of an original

Saxon fort or 'burh' built by Alfred the Great's remarkable daughter, Aethelflaed, in 914, as a defence against marauding Danes. She had founded a school in the castle – Warwick School - now in a splendid building on the south bank of the river, and laying claim to the title of the oldest boys' school in the country.

William installed Henry de Beaumont, the son of a powerful Norman family, as Constable of the Castle. Twenty years later his service was rewarded when he was made the 1st Earl of Warwick. Since then, the Earls of Warwick have been hugely influential in the governance of England, and indeed on more than one occasion decided whose head should bear the crown. The 12th century was in historical terms, a mess, with countless local wars breaking out across England and northern France. In 1153, Henry of Anjou, later to become Henry II, invaded to claim the English throne from Stephen. After all, he had a decent claim; Henry's mother Matilda was the daughter of King Henry I. And he had a powerful army, which is always a persuasive argument! Warwick Castle, loyal to the crown, was an obstacle to his ambitions.

Then it was in the hands of the 2nd Earl of Warwick, Roger de Beaumont. But he wasn't at home when Henry's troops arrived. His wife Gundreda was minding the fort. So Henry sent word to Gundreda that her husband was dead. She felt obliged to surrender control of the castle. According to a contemporary account, when Roger de Beaumont heard that his wife had handed over the keys to the castle, he promptly died – really this time! Later, when Henry had become the powerful King Henry II, he handed the castle back to the de Beaumont family. But women continued to get a raw deal as far as owning the castle was concerned.

In 1242, when the 6th Earl of Warwick, Thomas de Beaumont died, the castle, now fortified in Warwickshire stone with a barbican – a massive gateway – and two impressive towers, passed to his sister Margaret, the Countess of Warwick, who was married to John Marshal. But when he died shortly afterwards, with no man about the house, Henry III took ownership of the fortress until widow Margaret found a suitable husband. One of Henry's loyal knights, John du Plessis, fitted the bill. Margaret promptly married him and the castle was handed over to du Plessis, the 7th Earl of Warwick, and his Countess, Margaret. Clearly it wasn't acceptable for a mere woman to own a mighty castle.

Four hundred years later, under the ownership of Robert Greville, the castle was swiftly fortified further in preparation for the First English Civil War. The new bulwarks, barricades and machicolations, (also know as murder holes, where defenders could drop heavy stones or boiling oil on the enemy), were finished just in time. Robert Greville was a Parliamentarian, and on 7th August 1642 a Royalist force laid siege to the castle. When the commander of the castle garrison refused to surrender, the Royalists opened fire with two cannons that had been hauled up to the steeple of the nearby St. Nicholas Church. The cannon fire made little impression on the mighty walls of the castle. In fact it provoked the Parliamentarians to return fire. According to the Royalist nobleman Richard Bulstrode, "The cannon were discharged at the castle, to which they could do no hurt, but only frightened them inside, who shot into the street and killed several of our men." The siege was lifted after two weeks by the forces of the Earl of Essex, and the Royalists were forced to retreat to Worcester.

A Grand Day Out

These days, the castle is one of the top ten tourist attractions in the country, alongside the Tower of London and Stonehenge.

About 800,000 visitors each year enjoy a host of attractions offered by Merlin Entertainments. As well as the treasures and dungeons, there are elaborate shows of archery and jousting, with a Wars of the Roses theme. Amazingly skilful horsemen and women battle it out in the lists, with the crowd cheering the red rose or the white. The castle has a replica medieval siege engine called a trebuchet. When it's in action during the summer it can hurl a burning missile 300 yards across the Avon. Unfortunately on one occasion it hit a thatched boathouse which promptly went up in flames; a bonus for the spectators.

But for me, the best family show is a display of the castle's birds of prey. It's called 'The Falconer's Quest'. An actor on a raft on a branch of the Avon mimes to a narrative relayed by loudspeakers to the audience arrayed on the river bank, and one-by-one the birds appear, swooping to take food from a team of falconers. The delicate barn owl is first, suddenly appearing, white and silent, flitting between the rows of spectators. Then the birds become more and more impressive, with a peregrine hurtling through at well over 100 mph aiming for the falconer's lure, followed by a huge white-tailed sea eagle that glides so low over people's heads that children scream and duck. Even bigger is a condor. The downdraft of its wings makes your hair stand on end! The birds have all been bred in captivity, look very healthy, and seem quite relaxed in very close proximity to a crowd of admirers.

When I took members of my family there, including an open-mouthed granddaughter, two wild peregrines appeared circling very high above the river. I doubt if most of the spectators noticed them. The Warwick pair of peregrines use the tall tower of the Collegiate Church of St. Mary as their lookout and feeding post, and it's said they have nested somewhere on the castle ramparts. The falconers aren't saying.

Other birds the children will enjoy seeing are the castle peacocks, or to be accurate the peafowl – cocks and hens. The loud 'ceeow' of the peacocks can often be heard in Warwick. In May the males strut about on the castle walls, fanning their tails to impress the females, and occasionally fluttering down on to the streets and stopping the traffic. Originally forest-dwellers in India, peafowl have important places in most cultures and religions. In Hinduism the god of war, Lord Kartikeya, rides on a peacock, the chariot of the Greek goddess, Hera, was pulled by peacocks, and the exotic birds support the thrones of deities in Buddhist and Persian cultures. The peacock's fanned tail with its 'eyes' is supposed to represent an all-seeing god, symbolism adopted by the early Christians; many of their paintings and mosaics feature peacock feathers.

Historic Warwick

With the extensive grounds of Warwick Castle blocking the riverside, Shakespeare's Avon Way has to leave the river and go through the centre of the county town before rejoining the riverbank near Sherbourne on the way to another huge estate, Charlecote Park. But wandering through Warwick is a pleasure. It is compact, because when the castle was reinforced with stone in the Middle Ages, the market town that supported its garrison was surrounded by a high defensive wall. And even though only the Eastgate and Westgate survive, the centre of town is still defined by those long-demolished walls. The Westgate was also known as The Hanging Gate. The bodies of executed felons were left hanging there for weeks, to remind roving bands of brigands that they shouldn't mess with Warwick.

Attached to the Westgate is the Lord Leycester Hospital – one of the finest collection of medieval buildings in England. It was formerly the Guildhall of the burgesses who ran

Warwick. It's named after Robert Dudley, the Earl of Leicester, (spelled Leycester in the 16th century). He was the dazzlingly handsome favourite of Elizabeth I who entertained her lavishly, but never quite managed to gain her hand in marriage and therefore the throne. He was the younger brother of Ambrose, Earl of Warwick, and was based at Kenilworth Castle just five miles to the north. Robert acquired the Warwick Guildhall from the town's burgesses to become a 'hospital' - a rest home for retired army officers - by a clever ruse.

The Earl was due to receive the Order of St. George at St. Mary's Church in a grand ceremony. According to contemporary accounts, he had sent word ahead that he did not need to be greeted at the town gate by the trumpeters and burgesses, but they could wait at the market cross. He rode into town on a white charger wearing white clothes decorated with gold and jewels and wearing a huge plumed hat. But when there were no heralds or dignitaries at the gate he flew into a rage and, claiming to be disrespected, stormed off back to Kenilworth.

The Warwick guildsmen had to appease him. It was impossible to challenge the two most powerful earls in England, the brothers Ambrose and Robert Dudley. So the Guildhall was handed over, and in return the burgesses were give a tavern at the central crossroads for their mayor's parlour and meeting rooms. To this day, the 'Brethren', ex-military men, live in the former Guildhall, now the Lord Leycester Hospital, and show tourists around. The Town Council is still based at the site of the former tavern in a splendid building at the central crossroads called The Court House, because until the 1970s when a new Justice Centre was opened in Leamington, it contained the magistrates' court, formerly the Petty Sessions. It was built after the Great Fire of Warwick by Francis Smith and, like the Lord Leycester Hospital, is Grade-1 listed.

The Great Fire

Directly opposite 'The Lord Leycester', as it is known, is a row of Elizabethan half-timbered houses; then a few paces towards the centre of town, the architecture changes abruptly to brick and Georgian symmetry. It is impossible to understand the appearance of modern day Warwick without knowing about the impact on the town of The Great Fire of Warwick in 1694. At that time Warwick was a typical seventeenth century market town with narrow streets rammed with wooden-framed, thatched houses, shops, workshops and stables. September 5th was a very windy day. It is reported that a boy was carrying some hot coals from one workshop to another, opposite the Lord Leycester Hospital, when the wind whipped some sparks into the thatch of the cottages. The flames roared down the High Street, consuming in total 153 properties and destroying most of the medieval church of St. Mary's. The bells melted in the inferno as the church tower collapsed.

The Great Fire of Warwick, happening less than 30 years after the Great Fire of London, was regarded as a national tragedy and a public appeal raised substantial sums for the rebuilding of the town. Parliament also passed The Fire Act which laid down rules for future urban development. There would be no more narrow streets with combustible wooden-framed buildings and thatched roofs. Government Commissioners supervised the rebuilding of Warwick, with wider streets, and classically symmetrical buildings – the Georgian style much admired today. Much of the rebuilding was done by Frances Smith, known as 'Smith of Warwick'. He was a local builder who had made his reputation extending stately homes in the fashionable English Baroque style favoured by Christopher Wren, Nicholas Hawksmoor, John Vanbrugh and others, when they were erecting grand buildings after the great fire of London. This style was soon to give way to the plainer classicism known as Palladian architecture, which we tend to call Georgian.

Temple-haunting Martlet

Many of the big houses that replaced the smouldering ruins were built by 'Smith of Warwick'.

The result is a town with a mixture of half-timbered medieval and Elizabethan buildings that survived the fire, and elegant broad streets constructed afterwards in brick and stone. The Shakespeare Way takes us right though the Market Place with its County Museum, where the aforementioned plesiosaur is on show, along with a stuffed brown bear, one of the symbols of Warwickshire. And in contrast with the remains of dead creatures in the museum, the market place is full of lively little birds chirruping cheerfully over the stalls selling local produce.

The house martins have returned from their winter quarters in southern Africa to the nest sites where they were born, goodness knows how they navigated the journey. They have been glueing their mud nests under the eves of the 17th century Market Hall Museum for as long as anyone can remember. In folklore it's regarded as a sign that health and happiness will come to you if the blue and white house martins choose your house.

In Macbeth, when King Duncan and Banquo arrive at Macbeth's castle, they remark on the temple-haunting martlets (house martins). Their nest sites mean the air is sweet there.

Duncan: *This castle hath a pleasant seat. The air*
            Nimbly and sweetly recommends itself
            Unto our gentle senses.

Banquo: *This guest of summer,*
            The temple-haunting martlet, does approve,
            By his loved mansionry, that the heaven's breath
            Smells wooingly here...
            Where they most breed and haunt, I have observed,
            The air is delicate.

They have no idea what is going to befall them at the hands of their hosts. The audience, knowing that the story involves the murder of the king, can see the irony of them praising the sweet and delicate air at Macbeth's castle.

Screaming Swifts

And here's another bird that spends its life on the wing and nests under the eves of our houses - the dashing, soaring, screaming swift. This summer visitor is in steep decline as a nesting species in Britain. In just 25 years numbers have gone down by 53%. Fortunately, they still favour Warwick. The characteristic screams are a constant background sound in the centre of the county town as the swifts start speed-dating as soon as they arrive from Africa in May, and then compete for nest holes under the eves.

Swifts don't generally breed until they are four years old. So I wonder why the young birds bother to make the 5,000 mile journey from Africa, where there are plenty of flying insects in the summer. But it's clear something draws them back to the exact town where they were hatched, and it seems they are learning from the older birds. Sometimes called 'bangers', the younger birds have a habit of banging into a potential nest hole to see if it is occupied. If a hole has already been claimed the resident swift will come to the entrance and scream at them to clear off!

Swifts seem to like Warwick because there are still plenty of nesting places in the old buildings. Elsewhere in Britain the number of possible nest sites has fallen fast. Modern houses and those with new insulation to help with rocketing heating bills are not swift-friendly. In 2021 a coalition of the UK's leading bird conservation organisations moved swifts and house martins on to its red list of endangered breeding birds. The red list means that these species are of the highest conservation concern because of severe declines in numbers.

But there is an answer. Swift nest boxes are easy to buy online and they are quite easy to install under the guttering of any house. Builders of new houses are being encouraged to make them swift-friendly. It costs the builders next to nothing, and surely swift boxes can only help to sell a property. A petition launched in 2020 by Kerry McCarthy MP called for house builders to be required to fit swift boxes to new-builds. It soon reached 200,000 signatures. Unfortunately, the government ignored it.

It's a pity; swift boxes clearly work. A village in Devon, Drewsteignton, had no nesting swifts in 2000. A bird enthusiast moved into the village and started persuading everyone to put up swift nest boxes. In 2020 there were at least 26 breeding pairs. There's now a national campaign to get schools to install swift boxes. I think that is a great idea, encouraging these exciting birds to nest, but also introducing children to the fabulous world of nature.

June

Warwick to Charlecote Park

Shall I compare thee to a summer's day?
Thou art more lovely and more temperate:
Rough winds do shake the darling buds of May,
And summer's lease hath all too short a date.
(Shakespeare's Sonnet No.18)

Dunnock and Cuckoo

Stairway to Heaven

In Sonnet No 18, Shakespeare compared the constant beauty of his loved one with the all-too-transient summer days. It certainly seems to me that the summer months rush by while the winter drags its feet. So on our walk along the river path named after The Bard, let us revel in the high summer weather as we head for the beautiful Charlecote Estate.

Our way out of Warwick loops away from the river to circle round private land, but has some interesting features along the way. We leave town on the Birmingham Road, past Sainsbury's and the old gasworks, built in 1822 and now converted into flats, and we drop down to the Saltisford Canal Basin. This was the terminus of the Warwick and Birmingham Canal that delivered coke to the gas works and salt to the town, hence the name. Thirty years ago it was derelict. Thanks to a trust and a band of volunteers, it is now a thriving canalside attraction, with narrowboats for hire, a cafe and visitor centre. The towpath takes us north under the Warwick by-pass, and then we find ourselves faced with one of the great challenges of canal boating in England – The Hatton Flight.

Known locally as The Stairway to Heaven, it's not too heavenly to negotiate the Hatton Flight on a hot June day. It is a series of 21 locks which lift the Grand Union Canal 146 feet out of the Avon Valley to surmount a clay ridge leading up to Knowle, named such because it is on a hill – a knoll – before the canal heads on to Birmingham. In fact this great flight of locks was built twice. The original locks on the Warwick and Birmingham Canal were built in 1790 by the navigators or 'navvies' as they were known. The canal was renamed the Grand Union in 1929, and shortly afterwards new wider locks were built of concrete by a workforce of a thousand men.

The new locks were opened by the Duke of Kent in 1934; they can take two narrow boats side by side.

At the top of the climb you can stagger on to the Hatton Arms pub that has tables outside with a view across the fields, or cross the canal on a bridge which has a great view down the straight line of locks with the tower of St. Mary's in Warwick directly at the end. The Shakespeare way dips south through open farmland and the pretty village of Hampton-on-the-Hill, and goes under the M40 before heading due south to rejoin the river bank at Fulbroke Castle, now an earthworks. The castle itself is long gone. It was demolished during the reign of Henry VIII, and the nearby village was abandoned. It's a far too familiar story.

Ridge and furrow marks on the fields beside the Avon are all that remain of strip fields that once supported the village. Fulbrook was one of hundreds of villages devastated by the 'black death' in the mid-14th century. The bubonic plague killed almost half the population of Europe in a couple of years. But then Fulbrook was afflicted again in 1421 when the tenant farmers or 'villeins' were all forcibly evicted by John the Duke of Bedford so that he could enclose the land as a park for hunting deer. Little wonder then that crime in the area increased, with highwaymen terrorising travellers on the turnpikes around Warwick.

A World War II Hero

After carefully crossing the busy A46, the Warwick by-pass, we can see to the left of our track across the fields the village of Sherbourne. It had a noted son called Henry Eric Maudslay. There's a memorial plaque to him in the village church. In WW2 he was an intrepid bomber pilot who earned the Distinguished Flying Cross for his missions over Germany.

In 1943, Wing Commander Maudsley was selected to be commander of B Flight on Operation Chastise - the 'Dambusters' raid. The target of his Lancaster, Z-Zebra, was the Eder Dam.

The geography made the approach particularly difficult. When Z-Zebra's bouncing bomb was dropped it bounced too high and struck the dam's parapet. It's thought the resulting explosion damaged the aircraft. Squadron Leader, Guy Gibson, called out to Maudslay asking, "Are you ok?" To which the faint signal came in reply, "I think so. Stand by...", which was the last known voice contact with the aircraft. It was hit by anti-aircraft fire before crashing with the loss of the entire crew. Gibson wrote of Maudslay: "Henry was a born leader... a great loss, but he gave his life for a cause for which men should be proud. Boys like Henry are the cream of our youth. They die bravely and they die young."

Beyond Sherbourne, with the Avon looping round it, is the ancient village of Barford, spelled Bereforde in the Domesday Book, which probably means a shallow crossing point, or ford, good enough for a loaded hay wagon. Now you enter the village over a beautiful 18th century stone bridge with five arches. Unfortunately the old bridge and the village itself were often clogged with traffic until the Barford by-pass was opened in 2007. The Sunday Times promptly declared Barford as one of the top ten desirable places to live in Britain. It definitely suited Annie Butler who died there in 2009 aged 112; at the time she was the second oldest person in the UK.

It's certainly a lovely spot, with a village shop run by the community and featuring local produce, and the solidly built tower of the medieval church of St. Peter overlooking the meandering river. The tower has shot marks down one side, said to have been made during the Civil War, when Parliamentary supporters were marching towards Edgehill, and a local family hoisted a Royal Standard on the flagpole. The Roundhead soldiers tried to shoot it down, without success.

An Agricultural Hero

In the village there's a charming pub called The Joseph Arch, named after Barford's most famous son. He led a truly remarkable life, and without wishing to denigrate the bravery of the Dambusters' wing commander, I think Joseph Arch contributed more to British society in a very different way. He was born in Barford in 1885 and started work at the age of nine as a 'crow-scarer'. He became a plowboy for hire, and travelled around the midlands, noticing the terrible conditions endured by farm labourers. These were later described by the Countess of Warwick in the introduction she wrote to his autobiography.

'Bread was dear, and wages down to starvation point; the labourers were uneducated, under-fed, underpaid; their cottages were often unfit for human habitation, the sleeping and sanitary arrangements were appalling … In many a country village the condition of the labourer and his family was but little removed from that of the cattle they tended.'

Joseph Arch became a Methodist preacher and soon the workers turned to him for help. He arranged a meeting in The Stag's Head in Wellesbourne, just down the road from Barford. He expected about thirty people to be there. In fact two thousand agricultural workers and their families turned up. It led to the formation of the Warwickshire Agricultural Workers Union that very quickly became a National Union. He must have been a man of boundless energy and conviction. The union members withdrew their labour and achieved a pay rise from the landowners; but their success was fairly short lived as the union had few resources to support them on strike, and they had to accept the jobs offered by the lords of the manors.

Arch travelled to Canada and arranged for about 40,000 poverty-stricken British labourers to emigrate and start new lives in Canada and Australia. He also agitated for the widening of the voting franchise, which until then included only property owners, and the campaign resulted in the passing of the 1884 Parliamentary Reform Act. He became an MP, believing that was the best way to inspire change. He was the first agricultural labourer to enter the House of Commons. The farm labourers he championed sang songs in his praise:

> *Joe Arch he raised his voice, 'twas for the working men;*
> *Then let us all rejoice and say, We'll all be union men.*

It wasn't long before the workers thought he had 'sold out' to the establishment, and the ploughing songs changed.

> *Joseph Arch he stole a march, Upon a spotted cow.*
> *He scampered off to Parliament, But where is Joseph now?*

In 1900 he scampered off to retirement in his modest family home village of Barford where he lived another nineteen years. In my view, the former crow-scarer was one of the great figures of the late eighteenth century, inspiring much needed social change. It is only right that he is celebrated by a local group that organises a walk each June from Barford to Wellesbourne along a footpath called the Joseph Arch Way.

The Lark Ascending

On Shakespeare's Avon Way, our path drives south through open farmland and past another nature reserve, the Hampton Wood reserve of the Warwickshire Wildlife Trust. It's a damp spot next to the Avon, with rare lichens, lots of different fungi, and many insects including over 500 species of beetle. There are wetland plants including hemlock, creeping buttercup and the pale yellow meadowsweet. There's always the chance of seeing the lightning dash of the kingfisher here. But I'm pressing on across wide open fields towards the Charlecote Estate. On this sunny day there are puffy clouds and two skylarks are singing high overhead.

The continuous song of the skylark, with the bird apparently not taking a breath, has intrigued naturalists for many years. Ornithologists now know that connected to their single lung they have nine small air sacs surrounded by muscles that push them in like bellows while the bird is doing a form of circular breathing. Recordings of skylarks, greatly slowed down, has shown that they take 'mini breaths', which last for about thirty milliseconds - that's about a thirtieth of a second. The time it takes you to blink. These tiny breaths allow just enough air into their system to allow them to continue singing.

It's an uplifting sound, celebrated by writers over the centuries, including Shelley's famous tribute poem, 'To a Skylark'. And in his 29th Sonnet, Shakespeare refers to the uplifting sound of the skylark as a hymn at heaven's gate.

> *Yet in these thoughts my self almost despising,*
> *Haply I think on thee, and then my state,*
> *Like to the lark at break of day arising*
> *From sullen earth, sings hymns at heaven's gate.*

And listeners to Classic FM have voted 'The Lark Ascending' by Ralph Vaughan Williams their favourite piece of classical music for eleven years in a row.

Unfortunately our much loved skylark is in trouble. A predominantly farmland bird, it has suffered from multiple effects of more intensive farming. In the UK, the population halved during the 1990s, and is still declining. According to the RSPB, the main cause of this decline is considered to be the widespread switch from spring to autumn-sown cereals, leading to a dramatic reduction in the number of chicks raised each year. Autumn-sown cereals are taller and denser in the spring and summer. Fewer birds nest there, and those that do are unable to raise as many broods as birds nesting in spring-sown crops. Research shows that many nesting attempts are on or close to 'tramlines' (the tracks of the tractors that are used to apply the many sprays to the crop), which makes the nests vulnerable to ground predators.

As if that wasn't enough to put off the skylarks, autumn sowing means their winter food supply is also scarce in the absence of stubbles - favourite feeding areas. And the increased use of insecticides and weedkillers is likely to remove an important part of the food source. In grassland habitats, intensification has also been detrimental. Increased stocking densities on grazing land have made the grass too short for skylarks, and increased the risk of nests being trampled. A switch from hay to silage has resulted in many nests being destroyed by the cutting machinery, since the period between cuts is often too short for successful nesting. So the poor skylarks are under assault from many directions. I hope the various campaigns to make farming more environmentally friendly will encourage landowners to leave some rough grassland untouched to encourage ground nesting birds.

Charlecote Mill

The path follows a ridge with Copdock Hill to the right and splendid views of the river valley below to the left. There are grazing cattle half hidden in the long grass and water meadows.

It's a bucolic scene worthy of a painting by the greatly underrated painter, David Cox. Born in Birmingham in 1783 he produced hundreds of beautiful watercolour and oil landscapes, including many painted 'en plein air' in Warwickshire. Cox is regarded by art critics as a precursor of the impressionist movement. It seems to me a pity that his name isn't as well known as those of his contemporaries Constable and Turner. There's a fine collection of his work in Birmingham Museum and Art Gallery. One of his paintings is of Charlecote Manor, the next destination on our route.

Just outside the village of Hampton Lucy, a bridge over the Avon takes us to Charlecote Mill, one of just a handful of working commercial watermills remaining in the country. You can buy freshly milled flour there and have a guided tour of the working mill, but it is open for visitors on only a few days in the year, so you'll have to go to their website and book in advance if you want to see the only working watermill on the Avon.

There's probably been a mill here for a thousand years. In the Domesday Book the mill was valued at six shillings and eightpence. That's about 35p in today's currency, but a tidy sum in 1086 and an extremely valuable asset for the lord of the manor, who had the monopoly on grinding corn from the local farms. In the past millers weren't exactly popular. They had a reputation for fiddling three times over: the farmers who provided the grain, the customers who bought the flour and landowners who took a cut of the proceeds.

The description of the miller in Chaucer's Canterbury Tales is far from complimentary. He is described as a stout and evil churl fond of wrestling, with wide nostrils and hairs sprouting from a wart on his nose. And the tale he tells is crude, based on adultery and farting, in contrast with the Knight's Tale about chivalry that precedes it. And indeed, the Charlecote records tell us that in 1675 the miller, John Dickens, and three other men were indicted for 'the felonious stealing and carrying off two perches and two pikes to the value of elevenpence, of the goods and chattels of Richard Lucy Esq.' Dickens and Robert Nason confessed to pinching the sacks of flour, and were sentenced to be 'stripped from the waist downwards, (note, that's 'from the waist downwards' – can that be right?), and openly whipped through the town of Hampton Lucy till their bodies be bloody'.

Cuckoo

Ahead I can hear the unmistakable two-note call of a cuckoo. It's in the distance, but the soft call carries a remarkably long way. It is a real pleasure to hear a cuckoo these days because they have become uncommon hereabouts. Shakespeare notes that in his time they were so common they were "on every tree". And in Henry IV Part 1, the King warns that his predecessor Richard II, "was but as the cuckoo is in June, heard, not regarded." The sound of the cuckoo is certainly noticed now. According to the British Trust for Ornithology, the number of cuckoos in the UK has dropped 65% in just 40 years.

The reasons for this steep decline are not known, though scientists speculate that the target species of these parasitic birds are nesting up to a week earlier, and more cuckoos are missing their chance to plant an egg in the nest of an unsuspecting host. More likely is the fact that the journey to Britain from sub-Saharan Africa is getting more difficult, with a decline in their staple food, caterpillars, because the climate in Africa and southern Europe is becoming more arid.

Ornithologists have long wondered how a female cuckoo can change the colour of the egg it lays to match more closely the eggs of the host species. Now an international study led by the Norwegian University of Science and Technology has established that individual female cuckoos have distinctive genes that produce eggs of different shades, and each bird favours hosts that closely match the colour of her own eggs. The males that mate with many females – 'cuckold' behaviour in Shakespeare's time – make no difference to the egg colours. These colour genes are passed down only through the female line. Most cuckoo eggs are speckled, and range from an indeterminate greyish colour to light blue. The bluer eggs tend to be found in the nests of dunnocks, robins and reed warblers that lay light blue eggs. The cuckoo egg tends to hatch first, and the naked interloper proceeds to throw the other eggs out of the nest. The foster parents don't seem to notice this murderous behaviour, and frantically feed the huge foster child until it fledges.

Beautiful Charlecote Park

Further downstream we arrive at the entrance to Charlecote Park, for centuries the home of the Lucy family, and since 1946 run by the National Trust. That was when Sir Montgomerie Fairfax-Lucy presented the complete estate to the trust in leu of death duties. The Lucy family traces it lineage back to William the Conqueror himself, and they owned the land since 1247. It's a very large estate and deer park covering 185 acres, and is now a favourite for family days out. It's certainly one of my favourite NT properties, especially in high summer. A straight gravel drive leads to the original sixteenth century gatehouse, constructed in red Warwickshire brick. Beyond is the grand house.

You can book a tour of the house and see some elaborate plaster ceilings, hand painted wallpaper, fine wood panelling, works of art, and the room where Queen Elizabeth I stayed.

But I rather prefer the preserved below-stairs areas, with kitchens and washing rooms in a large outhouse; and then there are the grounds themselves, laid out by Lancelot 'Capability' Brown. The park is gorgeous, with a large herd of dappled fallow deer that delight the children, but unlike the deer at Richmond Park in London, they will not let you get too close.

There is a very persistent local legend that a young William Shakespeare was caught poaching deer at Charlecote, and was hauled up before Sir Thomas Lucy, the local magistrate and the landowner. Poaching was a serious offence, but according to this story, young William used his way with words to escape punishment. Another version of the story is that he abruptly left for London to avoid whipping. The tale crops up in no fewer than four biographies of The Bard written in the 18th century, and scholars point out that in The Merry Wives of Windsor, Justice Shallow – a vain and pedantic landowner - could be a pastiche of Sir Thomas Lucy. There is much play on words involving the 'luce' on Shallow's coat of arms, thought to refer to a louse, but when the character called Slender says to Shallow,

> *"...all his ancestors that come after him may: they may give the dozen white luces in their coat."*

the word *luces* would sound exactly like 'Lucys'. And 'luce' is the French for a pike; it's the fish symbol on the Lucy coat of arms. It is said that the Lucy family were so offended by these slurs that they tore the offending pages from the copy of Shakespeare's works in their library. Make of this what you will.

Behind the house flows the Avon, just below a terrace with the water meadows stretching away beyond the rippling river.

There are extensive lawns leading down to the river bank, a perfect spot for a summer picnic. The river itself is particularly lovely, with great fronds of water weeds waving in the clear water, and above a small weir the brown trout gather hoping for a crumb or two from your sandwich, their tails waving slowly to keep them in position in the fast flowing water. Standing on the bank I spot a kingfisher dashing past low and straight over the river, its orange chest reflected in the water.

Hobby

Above there are house martins and swallows. They suddenly start twittering their alarm calls, and high above them in the clear blue sky I can see a bird of prey like an anchor imprinted on the blue. It's a hobby, a small, agile falcon that migrates to Britain from Africa for the summer months, and feeds on dragonflies; but it will certainly take a martin or a swallow if it can surprise them. Its exceptional speed and agility means the hobby has been known to take swifts in flight. High over Charlecote Park I can see this falcon twisting and turning, clearly chasing a dragonfly that it catches in its claws, then nibbles off the wings that glitter in its wake.

At the end of World War II, the unfortunately named Peter Adolph was demobbed from the Royal Air Force and was wondering how to make a living. He adapted and improved a table football game called 'Newfooty', with cut-out players mounted on heavy buttons that could be flicked to play a plastic ball. He was a birdwatcher, and his favourite bird was the dashing little falcon, the hobby; so it seemed to him a neat idea to patent the new game under the name 'Hobby'. But that wasn't permitted by the Patents' Office, so instead he called it 'Subbuteo'. The Latin name for the hobby is *falco subbuteo*. The game flew off the shelves and is still popular to this day.

July

Charlecote to Stratford-upon-Avon

Why didst thou promise such a beauteous day
And make me travel forth without my cloak,
To let base clouds o'ertake me in my way,
Hiding thy brav'ry in their rotten smoke?
(Shakespeare's Sonnet No.34)

Red Kite

High humidity

The bright blue sky is suddenly obscured as July begins with sullen weather. Thick grey cloud has rolled in from the south-west bringing some bands of drizzle – not ideal for walking. It's 'close' as my parents would say, or 'muggy'. I wonder where these words came from? The word *close* appears in 16th century literature meaning in a closed and airless room, and is used in the modern way in the eighteenth century: "We had now for several days together close and sultry weather." (1748). The Oxford English Dictionary says *muggy* first appeared in print in 1746 as a northern dialect word meaning warm and humid. It suggests the origin is the Old Norse word, 'mugga' meaning a drizzling mist.

The Scandinavians have dozens of words for various weather conditions. 'Surt', literally 'sour' means it is bone-chillingly cold. And 'sludd' is the wet snow that melts as soon as it hits the ground, creating 'slaps' of slushy water. And how about 'bikkjekaldt' which literally means dog-cold, when it's so cold the dogs won't go outside. But in early July beside the Avon, it's definitely muggy. There are at least a hundred swifts over the river valley in a great cloud towering high against the grey ceiling like tiny crosses hurtling around. There's clearly an insect bonanza going on, possibly crane flies rising from the fields. At lower levels, flocks of starlings are also fly-catching and they are joined by three lesser black-backed gulls that stall in flight to take an insect. The fields by the river are adorned with meadow sweet looking like cream candy-floss, and the scent from the clusters of flowers is strong in the heavy air.

The following day there are crashing thunderstorms with shivers of lightning against the purple clouds. Bursts of torrential rain turn many streets in midland towns into mini Avons. Elsewhere in the world there isn't enough rain.

In western Canada, there are record high temperatures - up to 49.5 degrees celsius - and huge fires have broken out, consuming several villages. In Cyprus there are large fires in the Limassol area with British troops joining a vain attempt to stop the flames destroying some farmsteads. Most leading politicians now acknowledge that there will be more and more extreme weather events with devastating consequences if climate change isn't halted.

But soon the deep depression over central England moves away, the barometer unwinds, and the sun breaks through. We are soon in a mini-heatwave, but mainland Europe is suffering. The jet stream has looped around to the south of the British Isles and dumped unprecedented amounts of rain on western Germany, parts of France, Belgium and the Netherlands. Whole villages have been washed away.

Here in central England it is hot and calm as we leave the village of Hampton Lucy. Our path follows a lane due west with the river looping to the left, until we link up with it again at Hatton Rock. This is a vertical cliff with views across the valley to the village of Alveston. Ahead on the brow of a hill, is this a dagger I see before me? It's an enormous stone spike known as The Obelisk, constructed in 1876 by Robert Needham Philips in honour of his brother Mark.

The Obelisk

Now I'm not normally a fan of hilltop monuments built by rich landowners, dominating the landscape in a vainglorious display of self-importance. But I do rather like this slim, plain obelisk. And if you're going to celebrate someone's life, then Mark Philips' career would be more deserving than most. The son of a prosperous Lancashire merchant, he became Manchester's first member of parliament in 1832.

You may wonder why this thriving industrial centre had not been represented at Westminster before then. Once again, the English Civil War appears in our Avon story. After the restoration of the monarchy in 1660, Manchester was deprived of its parliamentary seat in reprisal for the town's support of the Parliamentarians. After more than a hundred and seventy years of non-representation, the Great Reform Act of 1832 granted seats in the House of Commons to the large cities that had sprung up during the industrial revolution, and removed seats from the 'rotten boroughs' - those with very small electorates and usually dominated by a wealthy patron.

As the first MP for Manchester, Mark Philips promoted many reforms, notably in the field of universal education, helping to establish publicly-funded schooling across the UK. He also promoted the establishment of public libraries. Philips was an active member of the Anti-Corn Law League, a political movement that campaigned successfully for the abolition of the unpopular Corn Laws, which protected landowners' interests by levying taxes on imported wheat. This raised the price of bread at a time when factory-owners were trying to cut wages. He also donated large sums of money to many social causes, including a thousand pounds towards the fund for open spaces and parks in Manchester. He moved to Stratford and in 1851 and became High Sheriff of Warwickshire.

So he probably deserves his massive obelisk, and the neighbouring Welcombe Hills Country Park is a great place for a midsummer day out, with fabulous views from the monument as far as the Malvern Hills. Looking out from the hilltop, with a pair of red kites slowly circling high overhead and the croak of a raven in the distance, one can see the differences in terrain on the north and south banks of the River Avon. The Elizabethan writer, John Leland, described the two areas of Warwickshire divided by the Avon. To the south of the river was 'The Feldon', including the flood plain. It was rich, corn-growing countryside. To the north was the Forest of Arden, mainly wooded with farmed clearings, and well known to Shakespeare, whose grandfathers had both been yeoman farmers in the forest.

The path on the approach to Stratford is a bit of a minefield. And a moving minefield. Dozens of froglets are hopping their way across the path heading for the ditch. It is difficult to place your foot without squashing a tiny frog. But my presence is probably saving a few lives. Many of the little frogs running the gauntlet would be picked off by birds if I wasn't there deterring them by my presence. But ahead along the path I can see a blackbird, picking up a froglet. Will it really stuff this into the gape of a young bird? ("I know you prefer worms, but try a bit of frog for a change?")

The Monarch's Way

Our path towards Stratford now joins The Monarch's Way. This is the second longest footpath in the country, winding for 625 miles from Worcester via the Midlands, Somerset and Devon, and ending at Shoreham on the coast of West Sussex. The monarch in question is Charles II, and the path follows his escape route after the Royalist forces were defeated by the Parliamentarians at the Battle of Worcester in 1651. It was the final battle of the Civil Wars marking the failed attempt by the young Charles to regain the throne after the execution of his father, Charles I. Yellow waymarker signs along the route have a crown and an oak tree, representing the time Charles hid in an oak tree while - according to Samual Pepys - Cromwell's soldiers rode past under the branch he was perched on. Also on the signs is a drawing of a sailing ship, representing Charles' escape to France from Shoreham harbour.

After crossing some open fields with meadow pipits bouncing away across the mounds of nettles and bramble, our way joins the towpath of the Stratford-upon-Avon Canal, opened in 1812 to connect Birmingham with the Avon. It required 54 locks and 3 aqueducts to travers the hilly terrain. Shakespeare's Avon Way arrives in the bard's home town at Bancroft Canal Basin in the heart of Stratford, with Bancroft Gardens on the riverbank overlooked by the Royal Shakespeare Theatre. The town is busy with theatre-goers, shoppers and canal enthusiasts throughout the year; but on a sunny day in July it's heaving with tourists. More than two and a half million visitors from all over the world come to Stratford each year, a testament to the global appeal of the plays penned by the son of a local glove-maker who found fame in London as an actor and dramatist.

The Shakespeare Phenomenon

I have to admit that as a schoolboy I found studying Shakespeare for English A-level a bit of a chore. The main problems were the antiquated language and the rather elaborate double meanings and references to things I didn't know about. But by the time I was studying English Literature at university, the light had been turned on. I had tuned-in to sixteenth century English, and realised that even though you might not understand all the references or clever word-play, the meaning and emotions came through. You knew that the characters were malevolent, naïve, cruel, stupid, ambitious, or crushed by unrequited love, even if some of the words or references were unfamiliar. And the stories were sensational!

In the plays, every scene of every act has a tension and some form of internal conflict. There is genuine philosophy in these plot-lines. The characters are known around the world – Hamlet the wronged but reluctant avenger; Lady Macbeth, urging her husband to murder the king and seize the crown but revealing her guilt while sleepwalking; Anthony obsessed with Cleopatra; the defiant but doomed Richard III calling for a horse at his final battle at Bosworth. And the plays are steeped in fabulous language. The courtly scenes are delivered in iambic pentameter – a form of poetry with five beats to the line – lending formality and elegance. The tavern scenes in Henry V are a very different style – much more realistic and with fast witty interplay. I find the comedies such as Twelfth Night, As You Like It, Much Ado About Nothing and A Midsummer Night's Dream, somewhat easier to follow than the History Plays and the Roman Plays. But they are all quite unreservedly brilliant. And of course The Tragedies – Hamlet, King Lear, Othello and Macbeth – are compelling, and, well, dramatic!

How could one man be so talented? And so prolific? Shakespeare wrote at least 38 plays and over 150 short and long poems, many of which are considered to be the finest ever written in English. I imagine him writing with a quill pen, often by candlelight. The first folio shows that he wrote down most of the lines first time. No delete button was available. His purple patch was 1599 – 1602, when he knocked off Henry V, As You Like It, Julius Caesar, Hamlet, Twelfth Night and Troilus and Cressida.

His works have been translated into every major living language, and some others besides; (the Folger's Holdings include translations in Esperanto and Klingon!). And more than 400 years after his death, the plays continue to be performed around the world. His birthplace just a few yards from the centre of town is one of the most photographed buildings in Britain, and his grave in Holy Trinity Church on the bank of the Avon is revered, almost like a shrine. He died on his fifty-second birthday. It seems Shakespeare was worried about grave robbers and people disturbing his bones. He wrote the following epitaph to be displayed above his grave as a deterrent, or a curse:

> *Good friend for Jesus sake forbeare,*
> *To dig the dust enclosed here.*
> *Blessed be the man that spares these stones,*
> *And cursed be he that moves my bones.*

It seems the curse didn't deter a certain Dr. Frank Chambers who is said to have broken into the grave in 1794 and pinched the Bard's skull, which he later sold for 300 pounds. In 2016, the 400th anniversary of Shakespeare's death, a team using ground penetrating radar was allowed to scan the grave. Sure enough, the skull that contained that fertile mind is missing! Alas, poor William.

Some say Shakespeare is overrated; he's a hype to attract tourists. I profoundly disagree. If anything he is under-appreciated because too many people think he is 'not for me' because the 16th century language is a barrier to meaning, and he seems to be the property of an intellectual elite. On the contrary, he spoke for the 'common man' in many ways, lampooning humbug. Of course he had to tread carefully when dramatising history – Queen Elizabeth wanted to hear that the Tudor family descendants were the rightful inheritors of the crown – so his Histories may not have been telling the real story. But that's not the point. He wasn't a chronicler, he was a playwright. And in many ways Shakespeare's plays are timeless, expressing our innermost feelings, fears, ambitions, envy, and love through brilliantly drawn characters.

Word, words, words

And the language! He was a poet, sensitive to cadence and imagery that have given us expressions we take for granted today. If your arguments are *baseless* and your opponent is *cold-blooded*, or if you *swagger* in *fashionable* clothes, or if your thoughts *vanish into thin air,* you are using Shakespeare's coinage, *for goodness sake!* Scholars say he invented no fewer than 1,700 words or phrases which have entered the mainstream English language.

In the centre of Stratford there is a splendid statue of the bard. At the four corners of his plinth are life-size statues of famous characters from his plays. How on earth did they choose just four? OK – Hamlet with his skull, contemplating death, is a cert. He represents philosophy and the central theme of our best writer – mortality. The History plays are represented by Prince Hal – later to become Henry V, the hero of Agincourt. There is Lady Macbeth, trying to wash the king's blood from her hands while sleepwalking. But who is on the fourth corner?

Falstaff. He is said to represent the Comedies, but, wait a minute. He appears not in the Comedy plays but in the Histories, and in many ways he is far from comic. He is cast by Shakespeare as cowardly, lying, and drunken – representing the life Prince Hal rejects to become a great leader of the nation. So I would have preferred to see Bottom the Weaver with an ass's head from the fabulous Midsummer Night's Dream on the fourth corner of the much photographed Shakespeare statue. The great man himself seems to be gazing not towards the Royal Shakespeare Theatre, but in the opposite direction towards the multi-story car park across the road. Perhaps he is thinking, 'the pay and display's the thing'.

Avian Flu

But all is not perfect in this perfectly lovely town in the heart of England. There are notices pinned to the benches beside the river warning people not to touch dead or dying swans and to call an emergency phone number to report them. While we humans have been grappling with a nasty virus, poultry and wildfowl have been afflicted by a new variant of bird flu, 'A-H5N1'. The UK's Chief Veterinary Officer, Dr. Christine Middlemiss, says the risk to human health is very low, but the virus can be devastating for poultry farmers.

Tens of thousands of farmed birds have been culled. But with the disease carried by wild birds, it's difficult to contain. Locals say that half of the famous swans that live on the Avon in Stratford have succumbed. It's not a pretty sight to see a once proud and stately swan sneezing and gasping. But these avian flu outbreaks happen periodically and one can only hope that bird numbers will recover over time.

Heading south-west along the path hugging the riverbank, we leave behind Stratford's big wheel. Yes, if you didn't know, Stratford has a big wheel, not quite as large as the London Eye, but big enough for my liking or disliking. I'm sure the view from the top must be impressive, but I'm afraid I'm not a fan of the domination of the skyline by this fairground ride in the centre of Shakespeare's Stratford. To be precise it is a Ferris Wheel, named after George Washington Gale Ferris Junior, who constructed one in 1893 for an Expo in Chicago. OK for an exhibition in Chicago. But in the centre of Stratford upon Avon? I'm not much in favour.

Our route out of Stratford passes beneath the walls of the splendid theatres, and Holy Trinity Church where Shakespeare's headless remains lie in dreamless sleep, and across a concrete footbridge to the south side of the Avon. For the next nine miles it will will stick close to the riverbanks though the villages of Luddington, Welford and Bidford into the lush Vale of Evesham.

August

Stratford to Bidford-on-Avon

Too hot, too hot!
(The Winters Tale. Act I Scene 2)

Yellowhammer

Climate concerns

The humidity of July has given way to cool, calm weather with a peppering of heavy showers from the west. It's more like April than early August, except most of the birds have fallen silent. Even the vocal wrens and robins are quieter than usual. The blackcaps, whitethroats and chiffchaffs are all keeping their beaks shut as they moult before migration time. Along the riverbank, the yellows and pale greens of spring have been replaced by a palette of purples. Great hairy willowherb, knapweed and purple loosestrife stand tall, but not as tall as the invasive Himalayan balsam that threatens to overwhelm the native species that favour damp ground. The tree canopies and the rushes below are beginning to look darker and dustier.

Soon the weather turns and it becomes very warm and still. Everything seems to be holding its breath. In other parts of Europe it's turning hot. Very hot. Italy and France are sweltering. 48.8 degrees celsius is recorded in Sicily - the highest temperature ever recorded in Europe. Wildfires in Greece are raging out of control. A flotilla of small boats is rescuing islanders and holidaymakers driven into the sea by a wall of flame. In Turkey fires have consumed several villages. According to the US Federal Scientific Agency measuring global trends, July was the hottest month recorded on Earth since reliable records began 142 years ago.

And then comes the 2021 report from the United Nations IPCC - the Intergovernmental Panel on Climate Change - the first major review by the world's top climate scientists since 2013. It is sobering reading. The report is headlined, 'Code Red for Humanity', and warns of extreme heatwaves, droughts and flooding in coming years, with rising sea levels inundating coastal cities, unless humans rapidly reduce their greenhouse gas emissions. The scientists weren't to know that Russia's invasion of Ukraine would require Europe to urgently find substitutes for Russian gas, including coal from the EU's eastern member states, newly licensed gas fields in the North Sea, and liquid gas shipped to Europe from the US – a reprieve for fossil fuels that I hope will be short-lived.

Round Trips

It's not too hot on Shakespeare's Avon Way. There's a pleasant cooling breeze and cotton wool clouds in a blue sky. We have joined the waymarked Avon River Walk that closely follows the bank awhile, with Stratford racecourse across the river to the right and some lush countryside to the left. I can hear some red-legged partridges chuntering in the cereal crop and there is a stock dove cooing soothingly in a tall willow. This stretch to Bidford is eight miles long and is a delightful walk along the river valley.

To the south there are wide fields of barley and wheat rippling in the breeze, and butterflies aplenty in the hedgerows beside the path, including some painted ladies that have migrated all the way from the desert fringes of Africa, the Middle East and parts of Asia. Until 2009, scientists didn't know whether or not these migrant butterflies return south in the autumn, or whether they perish here when the weather becomes too cold. But a major survey involving radar tracking showed that some adults and their offspring do indeed make the trip south in the autumn, flying at very high altitudes, so they are impossible to observe from the ground. It's a round trip of about 9,000 miles - pretty impressive for a fragile butterfly.

Talking of round trips, this is the start of the Avon Ring, a hundred-mile-long circular route much enjoyed by canalboat enthusiasts. Downstream from Stratford the river is a navigation, with seventeen locks between Stratford and Tewkesbury, where the boats join the River Severn, then travel upstream to link up with the Worcester and Birmingham Canal. From Birmingham the Stratford-upon-Avon Canal brings the traveller back to the start of the Ring.

In 2019, there was a bid to the District Councils in Stratford and Warwick, supported by the Avon Navigation Trust, to extend the ring by making the River Avon navigable from Stratford upstream to Warwick, where it would link with the Grand Union Canal. The cost was put at about £29 million. The councillors had to turn it down. 'Unfortunately in this case, the environmental and capital costs outweigh the benefits. We will however continue to work to improve public access along the river corridor between our two towns.' Certainly the riverside paths are kept in good condition along this stretch.

Dog Roses

Past the racecourse our route goes through a tunnel under The Greenway - a path and cycleway that is a former railway line. A footbridge takes us over the River Stour just before it joins the Avon, substantially swelling its waters. The hedgerows are embroidered with the last of this season's dog roses, looking like tissue paper flowers, now fading from pink to white, then fluttering on to the path like confetti. I've often wondered why they are called 'dog roses'. It seems that in days of old, the word 'dog' had a disparaging meaning in this context, indicating 'worthless' as compared with cultivated garden flowers. We also speak of 'dog violets' that are smaller than the cultivated version, and don't have the characteristic perfume of the sweet violet, *viola odorata.* But there's another theory.

The Roman naturalist Pliny believed that the name of the dog rose, *Rosa Canina,* came from the notion that it could cure the bite of a mad dog; and rose water was certainly used to treat dog bites in the 18th and 19th centuries. The wild rose is steeped in history and mythology around the world. The Greeks and Romans associated the rose with love and beauty, and it has become a worldwide symbol adopted by the nobility, including in Britain by the houses of Lancaster and York, and by the Tudors. And the bright scarlet rose hips, just forming in early August, are equally important in folklore. It is well known now that oranges and lemons are valuable for their vitamin C content. But for uncountable centuries, before the exotic citrus fruits were brought to Britain on trading ships, rose hips were the local source of vitamin C and more. These glowing red beads are pretty remarkable.

They are packed with antioxidants, mainly polyphenols and vitamins B and E as well as vitamin C, along with natural sugars, organic acids, polyunsaturated fatty acids, phenolics and essential oils. They are little health bombs! So it's hardly surprising that in Britain the rose hip has been used in a range of foodstuffs, including the well-known syrup, tea and marmalade. In central England they have been chucked into pies, stews and salads. During World War II, the British population, deprived of oranges because of the Atlantic blockade by U-boats, relied on rose hips and locally grown hops as their sources of Vitamins A and C. It was a wartime stiff-upper-lip expression to say, "We're getting by on our hips and hops."

Say Cheese

'A little bit of bread and no cheeeese'. Ahead along the path I can hear a yellowhammer repeating its song lamenting the lack of cheese for the ploughman's lunch. This interpretation of the yellowhammer's song became widely known in World

War II when hundreds of local cheeses became threatened with extinction.

With meat in short supply or expensive, the government promoted cheese as a nutritious alternative. But not any old cheese. Milk was redirected to factories to make a product that became known as 'Government Cheddar'. Promotional films were shown in the cinemas praising the virtues of the mass-produced cheese for the masses. 'Beef is not the only valuable food that the cow gives us.' The films quoted 'leading experts' saying that a piece of cheese weighing five ounces was as nutritious as a piece of beef weighing ten ounces. Ministry of Food leaflets claimed that, 'Cheese is an excellent body-builder, guards against infections, and helps you see in the dark!'

A decree was passed which banned the production of any cheese that wasn't 'Government' cheese. It's been estimated that at the beginning of the twentieth century there were 3,500 independent cheesemakers in Britain; by 1945 there were fewer than 100. The decree on cheese lasted until the end of rationing in 1954, and it took decades for many of our glorious regional cheeses to reappear in the shops. Perhaps the yellowhammer should be saying, 'A little bit of bread and plenty of cheeese, so long as it's Government Cheddar.'

Incidentally, why is this cheery hedgerow bird called a 'yellowhammer'? Most bird names come from their call, (chiffchaff), or appearance, (blackbird; blackcap), or the habitat when they are found, (marsh tit; reed warbler), or their native regions, (Mediterranean gull). A few are named after the ornithologists who first identified them, (Montague's harrier). But the common names of some birds go back many centuries to the Anglo-Saxon language known as Old English. For example, redstart means red tail, (*steort* in Old English). The name of the wheatear comes from the Anglo-Saxon 'white arse' because of the bright flash of white on its tail as the bird flies away. And 'yellowhammer' simply comes from the imported German word for a bunting – '*ammer*'.

Wild Swimming

Looking down the river I can see what appear to be two plastic balls floating on the surface, yellow and red. But strangely, they are not floating downstream but moving slowly against the current. They are bathing caps. Two women are 'wild swimming' in the Avon and cheerfully chatting as they gently breaststroke their way along the centre of the river. They aren't in wetsuits, just normal swimming costumes. I shout a hello and ask them what the water temperature is. "Oh, about sixteen degrees." They laugh. "There's nothing like it!" And certainly cold water swimming has become much more popular. The BBC News website declared in 2021, 'Wild swimming is Britain's new craze!'

According to 'Wild Swimming' magazine, (yes, there are websites and magazines devoted to cold water swimming), the Covid pandemic increased the number of people swimming in rivers and lakes by about 32%. Plunging into your local river complied with lockdown regulations, was very good exercise, and also connected you with your natural environment, which is a well-established way of helping you cope with mental stress. I resisted the temptation to strip off and join the two ladies on their swim in very cold water, and wondered just how healthy an activity wild swimming could be.

The problem is that our rivers are full of sewage. At least they are a lot of the time. Figures released in 2021 revealed that untreated human sewage was released into rivers in England on 370,000 occasions in the previous year. This usually happens after periods of heavy rain, when the water treatment plants can't cope and the untreated stuff is diverted into the nearest river. In addition, at any time of year, run-off from agricultural land can seriously poison our rivers. River pollution from farm land can happen in many different ways. Nitrogen-based fertilizers produce potent greenhouse gases, and they can also overload waterways with various pollutants that tend to reduce oxygen levels in the water and stimulate the growth of stifling weed. Run-off from poultry farms and pig farms can quickly kill off river life. Slurry from cattle sheds can dramatically reduce oxygen levels in the water.

It gets worse. Releases from industry are often devastating for our river network. For example, de-icing chemicals at the East Midlands Airport finished up draining into the River Trent, leading to a smothering fungus growing on the river bed. And there are quite frequent industrial accidents. A cleaning company inadvertently released cyanide into an angling lake at Shipley Country Park in Derbyshire. Unsurprisingly, the fish all died. So is it really a good idea to have a health-giving swim in the Warwickshire Avon?

At a meeting of my local Natural History Society, I have the chance to question an officer of the Canal and River Trust. "Would you go for a swim in the Warwickshire Avon?", I ask. He sucks his teeth and then says, "It's much cleaner than many other rivers, but - no I don't think I would - it depends what's been happening upstream." What he means is that if there's been a sewage release, stay out of the water! But how would you know?

Unclean Waters

As I write, the government has launched a consultation about river pollution. The trouble is the antiquated and leaking Victorian sewage disposal system can't cope with new housing developments and intensive farming methods, and there aren't enough treatment plants. The problem is severe enough for BBC Panorama to devote a whole programme to our polluted rivers, with countless examples of raw sewage being released, even when there are no heavy rain events. It seems it will take eye-watering billions to modernise the sewage network. The water industry also cites shortages of drivers and other staff for their inability to avoid wide-scale pollution of our waterways. But I note the private water companies are still paying generous dividends to their shareholders.

The Environment Agency, the regulator responsible for improving water quality in England, has recently issued a shocking report showing that most water companies oversaw an increase in serious pollution incidents compared with the previous year, leading to the Agency Chair, Emma Howard Boyd, calling for water firm chief executives to face jail. "Fines handed down often amount to less than a chief executive's salary", she complained. That's hardy surprising when you read that the annual salary of Severn Trent's chief executive rose by £830,000 in the previous year to £3.9 million.

For several years the environmental magazine called 'Ends Report' has been collecting some uncomfortable facts about the quality of Britain's rivers. Their deputy editor, Rachel Salvidge, says, "I wouldn't go swimming in a river in England in the same way that I wouldn't flush my head down the toilet". She recommends that communities should get their local river designated as a 'official bathing water site', which would oblige the Environment Agency to install a water monitor and take action if the readings are below acceptable levels. She says that there are just two registered river bathing sites in the country, compared with 1,300 lakes and rivers in France that are designated for safe swimming.

It seems the challenge is just too big to be confronted. Rachel Salvidge says that Defra, which sponsors the Environment

Agency, is loath to approve river swimming areas because pollution from untreated sewage, farms and industry, "... is so widespread that all of England's rivers failed to meet the legal standards for overall health the last time they were assessed." Doth the lady protest too much? After all, there are plenty of fish in the Avon, and otters are back in most of our rivers. But I think the watercourses could be thriving with much more wildlife, especially in the unseen depths where freshwater crayfish and mussels used to be prolific. And chemical pollutants can have long term effects on human health. For example, raw sewage can lead to high levels of e-coli in the water.

When the Environment Bill came before the House of Commons in October 2021, the amendments recommended by The Lords, which would have imposed a legal obligation on water companies not to pollute our rivers, were rejected by the governing Conservative party in the Commons after some intense lobbying by the water industry.

Action

The RSPB has issued a report on the state of our rivers called, 'Troubled Waters'. It notes the decline of biodiversity along our waterways and points the finger at non-regenerative farming practices, relaxed planning regulations, and inadequate sewage treatment systems. What can we do about it? A new organisation called 'River Action' is campaigning fiercely for water companies to uphold the law. They say that after years of improvement, the water quality of our rivers is now deteriorating. They blame chronic underfunding of the Environment Agency over more than a decade, and a reluctance to prosecute offending water companies.

But there are now some positive signs that the water companies are prepared to take action. Severn Trent, the main water provider in the Midlands, has pledged to accelerate efforts to protect rivers after the government and regulators called on the water companies to 'significantly improve their practices in England and Wales'. The Chief Executive of Severn Trent, Liv Garfield, admits, "The industry has not managed to keep pace with expectations". Well, I suppose that's one way of describing the regular release of untreated sewage into our rivers. She said Severn Trent would invest around £100 million each year to "reduce dramatically" sewage discharges.

The company has launched two large-scale pilot schemes covering about 35 miles of the rivers Teme and Avon; these pilots are running until 2025 when the results will be assessed. According to a policy document called 'Creating Bathing Rivers' published on Severn Trent's website, the measures include installing new disinfection equipment in six sewage plants, 'which will also tackle emerging issues such as pharmaceutical residues in the water', catchment management on about 370,000 acres of farmland to reduce what is called 'faecal pollution', (not a nice thought), and 'moving from infrequent overflow monitoring to providing real-time, open and extensive data on storm overflows and river water quality'.

And sure enough, grey metal boxes connected to perforated metal tubes in the water have appeared on the river banks in the Leamington and Warwick section of the Avon, with notices explaining that they are monitoring water quality. The aim of the project, says Severn Trent, is simple - the creation of the UK's first bathing quality river.

Craig Openshaw, a former lifeguard from Tewkesbury, is undeterred by the prospect of polluted water. It's reported that he has become the first person to swim the 47-mile navigable section of the Warwickshire Avon, raising an impressive £17,000 for cancer research. But he did admit to having an upset stomach.

Welford-on-Avon

As it happens, our riverside Avon Way passes a water treatment plant on the north side of the river before passing through Weston-on-Avon, a small village that was one of six hamlets given to Hugh de Grandmesnil by William the Conqueror as reward for his service at the Battle of Hastings. 'Merci, Hugh, 'ere are 'alf-a-dozen villages for you'. Before long, the path emerges on to the High Street of Welford-on-Avon, a ridiculously pretty and much photographed village, with brick houses, thatched cottages, and manicured front gardens loaded with pink and yellow roses.

There's a narrow hump-backed bridge crossing the Avon. To be precise, there is a small island or eyot in the river here and there are two linked bridges hopping across the two arms of the Avon. The bridge has priority signs for traffic, but you can't see if anything is coming until you reach the top. I watch as two cars come to nose to nose, and one, (on the non-priority red arrow side), reverses.

There is a large sign pronouncing in capital letters, WEAK BRIDGE. With a 10 ton limit for lorries. I watch as a double-decker bus bound for Evesham hoves into view and climbs over the bridge. How heavy is a bus? I look it up. 12.65 tonnes apparently. That's 12.45 British imperial tons. The bridge survived.

Riverside Dining

Next to the bridge at Welford stands a large gastro-pub called The Four Alls. Its outdoor dining area is protected from any unsettled weather by large cream-coloured parasols and awnings, and in the summer it's an idyllic spot. The river is lazy here, with weeping willows brushing the surface of the water, lush rushes, and rafts of yellow water-lilies. A green woodpecker laughs casually nearby and grey wagtails are collecting flies to feed to their begging youngsters on the pebbles at the water's edge. Swooping over the river are agile birds of brown and white, nesting in crevices in the ancient bridge. It's a colony of sand martins, chirruping happily as they collect insects. Their chicks in the stonework will be their second broods of the year, and not long after they take flight, they'll have to feed up ready for the long trip to The Sahel, south of the Sahara, to avoid the North European winter.

I ask the welcoming young woman at the reception desk, why it's called 'The Four Alls'. She immediately ushers me into the ladies' loo! "Let me show you something". I'm getting nervous. But no need. Waving her arm like a conjurer's assistant, she demonstrates a row of four stained-glass windows. They show a king, a priest at prayer, a knight and a workman. They are in Victorian style, and represent an old aphorism. The figures are said to mean, The King rules for all, the Priest prays for all, the Knight or Soldier fights for all, and the Ordinary Man pays for all.

Images of The Four Alls go back to medieval times and seem to be a bitter definition of feudalism from the peasants who pay for all. The early Methodists adapted the Four Alls to indicate to the downtrodden workers that salvation from their unhappy lot could come only from Christ. Their version was, 'All need to be saved. All may be saved. All may know that they are saved. All may be saved to the uttermost, (without limit).'

Welford's main claim to global fame was that it had the tallest maypole in the world. Unfortunately, a few years ago, the original wooden pole, (dating back to Shakespeare's time apparently), was struck by lightning and was replaced by the present metal version, painted in red, white and blue stripes, and standing more than 60 feet high. It's a Grade-2 listed erection, but now downgraded from the world's tallest to one of the tallest in England. I wonder where in the world they have a taller maypole. We may find out very soon.

Bidford-on-Avon

The Shakespeare Avon Way now leads us west along one of the most attractive and peaceful stretches, hugging the south side of the river bank for three miles. Pilgrims's Lock and Weir is a lovely spot for stopping by the whooshing water for that packed lunch in the shade of the weeping willows. Or hang on, and treat yourself to a superb lunch at the aptly named, Cottage of Content, in the next village downstream, Barton. This is another pretty hamlet with timber-framed cottages and carefully tended gardens. Crossing it is The Heart of England Way, one of several long-distance footpaths criss-crossing the Midlands. This one is a north-south route over 100 miles long, starting in Bourton-on-the-Water in the Cotswolds, then skirting the Coventry and Birmingham conurbations, to end on Cannock Chase in Staffordshire.

As I approach Bidford, the blackbirds and wrens suddenly start shouting their alarm calls. A predator is about. Sure enough, a sparrowhawk comes from behind me quite low over the centre of the river with its characteristic flap-flap-glide motion. And there's another! The smaller male is following the female, slightly above. I have read about sparrowhawks hunting in pairs but have never seen it before. The theory is that the larger female panics birds to fly up and away, and the more agile male picks one off as the prey is watching the female.

The sparrowhawk pair disappear down stream and soon the track arrives opposite Bidford-on-Avon, where a buttressed bridge with seven arches takes you across the river. The old bridge is narrow and there's a one-way traffic lights system.

I wonder what would have happened in medieval times when two carts met in the middle. Bidford is a lovely town with the main road far enough away from the riverside not to disturb the peaceful setting. The High Street is narrow, with stone and half-timbered buildings. A pub called 'The Frog' stands by the river, and beside the bridge, there's a pub restaurant called, rather obviously, 'The Bridge'. On the south side of the river there are wide views across the Avon flood plain to a low line of trees more than a mile away.

Another raptor is in view, apparently nailed to the blue sky. It's a kestrel, hovering over the long grass watching for voles or mice. There's a cricket pitch and a row of picnic tables on the river bank in this classic English scene. Across the road is the 'Balti Hot', and next to it a 'Fine Indian Dining' restaurant, and 'The Avonside' – a Chinese takeaway. All culinary tastes are catered for in Bidford.

The town also seems to have more than its fair share of barbers and hairdressers. Maybe the clean air encourages hair growth. Here is 'Billy Shears'. I like that, but non-Beatles fans may not get the reference to the opening track of Sgt. Pepper's Lonely Hearts Club Band. If you haven't heard it, throw down this book and go and listen to it! Hairdressing salons and barbers seem to be particularly creative in naming their businesses. 'It's a Snip'; 'A Cut Above'; 'Scissor Sisters'; 'Head Girls'; 'Heads You Win', etc. (I'm not too sure about 'Hair Today'). But certainly in these difficult times, hair care is a business that is sure to keep on growing.

September

Bidford to Evesham

Gonzalo: *How lush and lusty the grass looks! How green!*
Antonio: *The ground indeed is tawny (brown).*
Sebastian: *With an eye of green in 't.*
(The Tempest, Act II Scene 1)

Blackbird and Rowan

Grass

There is a large high pressure area sitting over the British Isles. It has been there for nearly 4 weeks. August was generally grey in central England, with a few bright sunny days, but with light winds throughout the month. September has brought something of an Indian summer for a few days at least. The newspapers call it a 'mini-heatwave', but it's pleasant enough for walking. It's a distance of about eight miles from Bidford to Evesham, but there are plenty of villages along the way where one can pause awhile. The river and the path alongside dip south towards the village of Marcliff. There is a series of small wooden bridges over the drainage channels and streams feeding the river from the flood plain, which has tall grasses waving in the breeze, more brown than green I would say, Gonzalo. Then the path passes over some rising ground with the river below on the right, and there are some super views across the river valley and the Vale of Evesham.

There are 11,400 known species of grass in the world, and many more varieties or sub-species, from bamboo in China to scrubby short grass in the tundra of the sub-arctic. Without grass we would be in big trouble. Grasses are regarded by botanists as the most important family of plants for the survival of humankind, with about a fifth of the land surface of the planet covered by varieties of grass. Of course, cereal crops are a form of grass, and the meat we eat comes mainly from herbivores. Grasses also break down the soil and prevent massive erosion.

Here I can see lots of different types, and I don't know what most of them are. But there are few I can recognise. The meadow barley is quite prominent and easy to notice. It has bristles like its cultivated cousin that flavours our beer, and it ripples pleasingly in the breeze, seeming to copy the nearby surface of the river. Many grasses common in Britain have charming names, such as Yorkshire Fog, Foxtail, Cocksfoot, Common Couch, Quaking Grass and Crested Dog's Tail. Our forebears knew the importance of grass and the merits or disadvantages of different varieties.

Hedges

Alongside the path and skirting the fields with their grassy fringes are some mature hedgerows of hawthorn, blackthorn, hazel and ash. When environmentalists ask questions about the loss of so many farmland species post-war, especially insects and the birds that eat them, the loss of hedgerows figures large in the analysis. In the 1950s, '60s and '70s, farmers were encouraged to create larger and more productive arable fields to increase food production. It's thought that about half of Britain's hedgerows were uprooted in those three decades at a rate of about three thousand miles of hedge each year. It was a pretty ghastly period for conservation. Barbed wire or electric fences might be low-maintenance substitutes for controlling livestock, but the grubbing up of hedgerows has created biodiversity deserts. Not only are there fewer places for birds to nest and find food, but hedgerows are a network of wildlife corridors, connecting spinneys, woodlands or wet places.

But there is now some better news. In 1997, Hedgerow Regulations were introduced to protect 'important' countryside hedges. It is against the law to remove most countryside hedges without permission from the Local Planning Authority (LPA) who, on request, must determine if a hedgerow is important. The LPA is unlikely to grant permission to remove an important hedgerow. So hedges are no longer being ripped up indiscriminately. But the challenge now is how to replace those that have been lost over the years? It can be expensive for any hard-pressed farmer. But the National Hedgelaying Society reports that demand from farmers for new hedges is exceeding their ability to provide qualified hedge-layers. It's a skilled job. You don't want your new hedge to dry up and die within a couple of years.

So the society is appealing for more young people to take apprenticeships and learn this ancient craft. The hedge-laying season is from September to April, when the hedgerow birds are not trying to raise their young. The government recently announced a grant of up to £24 per 100 metres of new hedgerow. Yes, I know, a £20 note for every 100 metres is gesture politics; but at least it recognises the wide desire to bring back our hedgerows.

Nigel Adams sits on the Hedgelink steering group that advises Defra. He says there has been a recent sea-change in attitudes with everyone from the Farmers Union to Natural England calling for more hedges. "Suddenly everybody is realising that hedgerows are the veins of our countryside." He points out that as well as acting as wildlife corridors, they also help to tackle climate change. They soak up more carbon than a fence, and provide important protection against flooding and soil erosion.

The Magical Rowan

Hedgerows also produce a wide range of wild fruits. When we were a largely rural race, we humans would be out with baskets and bags in September, collecting the fruit to make jams and jellies for the winter. Along this stretch of the path there are mounds of bramble, loaded with blackberries, sloes on the blackthorn, and some crab apples. And further ahead I can see some bright red clusters of berries against the blue sky. There are three rowans standing tall in the hedgerow, their fingered leaves trembling in the breeze. The clusters of berries are bright scarlet. They are rather bitter to the taste, but are traditionally paired with apples to provide a sweet jelly. The berries are high in pectin that helps the mixture to gel, and are a good source of dietary fibre.

The rowan, also known as the mountain ash, is not only a lovely looking tree, it is steeped in European folklore. It will protect you. In Norse mythology, when the god, Thor, was being swept along a river towards the underworld, he grabbed a rowan branch bending over the water and was saved. Early Scandinavian myths tell how the first woman was made from a rowan tree; the first man came from the less attractive but stronger and taller ash tree.

In Greek mythology, Hebe, the goddess of youth and cupbearer to the gods, was busy moving among them, dispensing rejuvenating ambrosia from her chalice, when guess what? Some demons pinched her cup. Oh no! The gods were far from pleased and did what anyone would do if robbed by demons. They sent over an eagle to get back the chalice. There was an aerial battle and the eagle lost some feathers and drops of blood. Wherever they fell to earth a rowan tree sprang up. That's why the rowan's leaves are shaped like eagle feathers and the berries are like droplets of blood.

In the British Isles, particularly in Scotland, the rowan continues to have a place in popular folklore as the tree that protects against witches and demons. This belief may well be because each individual berry has a neat five-pointed star opposite its stalk. It's a pentagram, an ancient magical symbol with protective powers, going back thousands of years BC. The five points of the star are said to represent many things, including the five senses, the five fingers on the hand and in Christian times the five wounds of Christ. In the brilliant fourteenth century poem, 'Sir Gawain and the Green Knight', the young Gawain from Arthur's Court has a pentagram on his shield and a picture of the Virgin Mary on the inside as he sets off to meet his doom. Protected by the pentagram, he lives to tell the tale of his encounter with the green axeman.

And the autumn rowan displays even more powerful symbols. In former times, the colour red was the best protection against magic and demonic power. There's an old country rhyme recorded in collections of folklore:

> Rowan tree and red thread
> Makes the witches tine [lose]
> Their speed.

So the colour red will obstruct the malevolent spirits that stalk the land. To this day, some country dwellers plant rowans near their front door to afford protection against evil. And this amazing tree is used in many practical ways; the strong wood is good for carving and was used for walking-sticks and spinning wheels. It's said that a dye made of bark and berries was used by the druids to decorate their cloaks. Even now, from Scotland to Cornwall, some country-dwellers sew into their clothes crosses made of rowan twigs and bound with red thread. It may not come as a surprise that in Scotland the berries have also been used to make variety of alcoholic drinks, including a strong spirit and Rowan Wine, still made in the Highlands. Wild rowan jelly continues to be popular north of the border and is traditionally eaten with game.

The Vale of Evesham

Fruits of the cultivated kind are coming into view now. The Avon Way leaves Marcliff on rising ground across a series of fields with stiles and kissing gates before rejoining the river on a high bank with the flood plain stretching away on the opposite side to the north. Ahead are straight rows of fruit trees and wide fields of vegetables, some already ploughed for the next season. For we have slipped across the county border into Worcestershire, and this is the Vale of Evesham, the 'vale' being of course the valley of the Avon where it widens after being joined from the north side by the River Arrow.

To the left is the handsome church tower of Cleeve Prior. Wherever there is a fine church in a relatively small village, one can be sure it was part of a rich rural economy. In some parts of the country, wool made the manor affluent and the manor church well endowed. In this case it was the rich loamy soil of the Vale and the fruit and vegetables that were transported down the river to Evesham and beyond that brought the wealth to the area, and in particular to the Priors of Worcester who had owned much of the region since Anglo-Saxon times, hence the name of the village. The 'Cleeve' part comes from the Old English for 'cliff', because the village is on the high ridge of limestone overlooking the valley, and safe from the floods that can cause mayhem around here.

Bounded by The Cotswolds, Bredon Hill and The Malverns, the sheltered valley was famed for its fine produce for hundreds of years. It was called the 'Eden of Fertility'; and the 'Garden of England', though Kent also claimed that title. But it was the engineering revolution and then the technology revolution that have boosted it fortunes in the past 200 years. As the populations of Birmingham and the Black Country expanded rapidly, so did the demand for fresh food for the indoor markets erected in Digbeth and Dudley. London's Covent Garden and Borough Markets needed more and more supplies too.

So two separate railway companies extended their lines to Evesham in order to deliver the fruit and veg overnight to the big towns and cities. The Oxford, Worcester and Wolverhampton Railway opened its station in 1852, and sixteen years later, the London Midland line opened its station right next door. The market gardens in The Vale kept on expanding and the trains to Birmingham and London were loaded with plums, apples, pears, cherries, gooseberries and strawberries, as well as a variety of green vegetables.

Then came the supermarkets, with their purchasing power and ability to import fresh food when it was out of season in Britain. So the Vale of Evesham had to go high-tech. There are still small growers in the Vale, but now there's a much larger industrial-scale horticultural sector with glass and plastic glittering across the landscape, huge robot machines watering automatically when the soil becomes dry, and investment in the varieties that bring most profit per acre. Asparagus is a good example. It has become a mainstream vegetable in the shops, and in The Vale more than 2,000 acres are now devoted to this prized crop, providing no less than 65% of all the UK's asparagus. New strains mean it can be grown much longer than the traditional season, (St. George's Day in late April to Midsummer's Day in June). Tomatoes are now grown 'hydroponically'. That's a relatively new system where the plants are grown under glass in water laced with nutrients, and without any soil! Sounds weird, but planted, (or should that be dropped into the bath), in January, they produce tasty tomatoes until November.

Offenham

The riverside path takes us through some wooded sections and a caravan site, before passing the inviting Fish and Anchor Inn and into open fields as the Avon curves away to the north. We are entering the village of Offenham, bordered by a loop in the river and surrounded by nurseries and market gardens. The name is thought to refer to King Offa of Mercia. He was the Anglo-Saxon ruler of the Midlands in the 8th century, and no doubt would have expected a decent supply of fruit and veg from this 'ham' or hamlet in the heart of the growing area. It's said he had a house in the village.

The fifteenth century church in Offenham is dedicated to St. Mary and St. Milburgh. So who, you may be wondering, was St. Milburgh, (or Mildburh or Milburg in some records)? She was a noblewoman and an abbess at a retreat in Shropshire. Known for her humility, she had a lot of talents. She could heal the sick and restore sight to the blind. But notably she had a mysterious power over birds. When she humbly asked them to stop damaging the crops, they would obediently leave, which was quite a handy talent in a time before explosive bird-scarers or guns, and good enough reason for the farming families in the Vale to pray to her to keep the birds off their crops.

At the end of the main street in Offenham is a striped maypole – the second we have encountered on this trail. This is not any old maypole. It is 64 feet high, just a little taller than the one in Welford-on-Avon, and the tallest of only six maypoles remaining as permanent structures in the whole of England. What the maypole represented, and why the dancing with long ribbons survives to this day is – to be perfectly honest – shrouded in the mists of time. But the tradition seems to have come to Britain from Germany, and certainly has something to do with matchmaking, as well as celebrating springtime. Leaving Offenham and its tall maypole behind, you may hear the unmistakable chuff-chuff and poop-poop of a steam engine, for across the river is the Evesham Vale Light Railway, running for a mile through a Country Park and some attractive fruit orchards. Operated by a devoted team of volunteers, the railway has half a dozen beautifully maintained locomotives, and is a lovely ride at anytime of the year, though blossom time is probably the best.

Bird Sounds

Our path crosses the busy A46 Evesham By-Pass and approaches Evesham itself. Towards the end of the month the weather has turned colder, with clear skies. Suddenly it feels very autumnal, with the smell of fallen leaves and the rasping sound of jays collecting acorns and chestnuts. A thin, high-pitched peep overhead means that the first redwings are arriving after their long journeys from northern Scandinavia and Russia. Alongside the trail the robins are tic-ticking at anyone walking past. Their scolding seems to be particularly loud in the autumn. How does the robin produce that high-volume metallic sound without spraining its larynx? The answer is a bird's larynx doesn't produce its calls or song at all. That comes from the syrinx, found lower down, just above the lungs that act as bellows squeezing air through vibrating membranes and tubes.

The language of birds has often been studied by ornithologists. The robin's loud tic-tic is thought to alert other birds to the presence of interlopers on the ground, such as cats, dogs and humans. But if the danger is above, for example a crow, magpie or sparrowhawk, the robins will emit a very high-pitched 'seee seee'. Blackbirds will produce a similar warning whistle. I know from experience that this note is very difficult to locate. A recent experiment in the US with captive red-tailed hawks and owls, showed that when the seee-seee call was played to them, their heads turned in various directions as they tried to hear where the sound was coming from. Apparently 84% of the time they were looking off-target, unable to say where the sound was originating.

The different alarm calls of birds were a special interest of the ornithologist, writer and broadcaster, Jeffrey Boswell, who died in 2012. Over fifty years ago he helped to found the natural history section of the National Sound Archive based in the British Library in London. It has about a million and a half audio discs and tapes, as well as countless digital audio files. I reckon most of us have little idea how many messages there are in bird calls. I've learned to identify some alarm calls. For example, when crows spot a buzzard they emit a guttural croaky call, and if a sparrowhawk is around, starling will all start shouting 'pink-pink-pink'. But much of the language of birds is a mystery to us humans.

Michaelmas

By the end of the month most of the blackberries have gone, eaten by birds, and those that remain are not recommended. According to folklore, blackberries shouldn't be eaten after Michaelmas Day, September 29th. This is the day in the Christian calendar that commemorates the moment the Archangel St. Michael expelled Lucifer from Heaven. The Devil fell straight into a blackberry bush. He then cursed the fruit, scorched the berries with his fiery breath, and spat and stamped on them. Some say he urinated on them in his rage; so certainly blackberries in October are to be avoided! Michaelmas Day is the traditional beginning of autumn when there are plenty of other fruits and nuts to be gathered in the hedgerows for the winter, and it's harvest time in the orchards.

October

Evesham to Wyre Piddle

The teeming autumn, big with rich increase,
Bearing the wanton burden of the prime,
Like widow'd wombs after their lords' decease.
(Shakespeare's Sonnet 97)

Kingfisher

Asum Grammar

Our way through the 'teeming' orchards of the flood plane crosses the Avon on an elegant three-arched bridge into the ancient market town of Evesham. Or is it 'Eve-e-shum' or 'Eve-uh-shum'? Many of the locals still pronounce the name in three syllables; some compress it into 'Ashum'. Until quite recently there was a distinctive dialect spoken in these parts by a few old-timers. It's called 'Asum Grammar'. According to a glossary of Worcestershire words and phrases published at the end of the nineteenth century, a writer on dialects identified only as Mrs. Chamberlain had noted that the language of the 'old Worcestershire folks' in the Evesham area was 'interesting and peculiar'. But even then it was in decline, and these days the dialect is little more than an accent - but quite a distinctive one.

Those who are old enough to remember Walter Gabriel in the long-running BBC radio series, 'The Archers', will have been hearing an approximation of the South Worcestershire accent from Chris Gittins, who played Walter for 35 years. For this area is the setting for the fictional county of Borsetshire. Several places have laid claim to being the model for Ambridge, including Hanbury and Cutnall Green, but perhaps Inkberrow has the best claim because of its pub. 'The Bull' in Ambridge is said to be modelled on 'The Old Bull' at Inkberrow. And there's a family brewery in the village producing 'Ambridge Ales'. Chris Gittins came from Stourbridge, eighteen miles away from Inkberrow and the supposed Ambridge location. Near enough, you might think. But purists from Evesham complained that his oft-used phrase, 'Oh dear oh lor', came from miles away in the heart of the Black Country! Oh lor!

Evesham

Evesham is a very attractive town with a wide High Street lined by a variety of characterful buildings, some of them more than seven hundred years old. The town's origins are much older than that. It was founded in about 700 AD inside a horseshoe-like loop of the River Avon by Saint Egwin, the Bishop of Worcester. It seems that a swineherd called Eof had been tending his pigs by the river when he saw a vision of the Virgin Mary. This was reported to the bishop who went to see for himself, and the same vision appeared. He took this as a sign that an abbey should be built on the spot. The place was recorded as *Eveshomme* in 709, which in Old English meant Eof's meadow, and by the time of the Domesday Book in 1086, it had become *Evesham*.

The Abbey was destroyed by Henry VIII's men during the dissolution of the monasteries, but the magnificent bell tower remains in an area of parkland close to the town centre. Nearby is the Abbey Church that contains the grave of Simon de Montfort, or should I say some of the remains of Simon de Montfort, because after the Battle of Evesham, his body was right royally dismembered. He occupies a central place in our medieval history during the turbulent and violent time of the Barons' Wars, when some of the powerful regional earls rose up against King Henry III for failing to honour the terms enshrined in Magna Carta, and for giving them a raw deal financially. I'll have a look at the site of the famous Battle of Evesham before continuing on the path downstream.

Here in the centre of town just beside the old Market Hall, I spot a blue plaque. Perhaps it will mark the birthplace of a politician, poet or prince. No, it's Jim Capaldi! He was born here in 1944 and died at the age of sixty. He was one of my pop music heroes who played with all the big names in the

1960s - Clapton, Hendrix, Harrison and many more. He was one of the founders of the innovative band, 'Traffic', and was a fine drummer and guitarist as well as a lead singer. He was christened Nicola, after his Italian grandfather, which must have been a handicap at school; but he did more than alright. After all, John Wayne was christened Marion.

From the centre of town there are extensive areas of mown grass called Abbey Fields and Ferry Fields leading down to a riverside walk lined with lime trees, and with plenty of brightly-painted narrowboats and cruisers tethered along the banks. There are rows of Canada geese and mallard perched along the edge, socially distanced, and preening as they lose the last of their moulting feathers. On the other side there's a kingfisher perched on a mooring rope, occasionally bobbing its head as they do. Then it's off, with the distinctive high-pitched 'peep'. The riverside path to the west stretches for about a half a mile beside the lethargic river to the Hampton Ferry.

The Hampton Ferry

This crossing point dates back to the 13th century when the monks of Evesham Abbey needed a direct route to their vineyards on the sunny bank opposite; yes - vineyards in the middle of England. Climatologists have discovered that there was a period of nearly 300 years up to the middle of the 13th century when Northern Europe was unusually warm.

They call it the Medieval Warm Period, (MWP), when glaciers in Iceland and Norway shrank, and the Vikings exploited the ice-free northern waters to colonise Newfoundland, Greenland and almost certainly the east coast of America two centuries before Christopher Columbus. The MWP was followed soon after, from about 1400 – 1700, by the European Little Ice Age, and that's also known in scientific circles by its acronym, LIA. The Baltic Sea froze, and in 1658 a Swedish army marched across the ice to attack Copenhagen in Denmark. In London, there were parties and skating on the Thames.

The Hampton Ferry is a cable ferry, with the shallow boat hauled across manually. A notice says it is £1 to cross. Very reasonable. But there is no way of summoning the boat. I can see the burly boatman on the far bank. He's just brought out a pint of ale and is sitting at a table on a lawn by the ferry house. Fair enough. It must be hard work pulling on those cables. Maybe I'll do likewise and have a beer in the garden of Raphael's Restaurant overlooking the ferry. Half an hour later there is no sign of the ferryman coming over to my side, so I give up and head up a straight path through the centre of town to the blood-soaked fields of The Battle of Evesham.

The 'Murder' of Evesham

In the thirteenth century, Simon de Montfort, a French nobleman who was the 6th Earl of Leicester, had become a close advisor to King Henry III; marrying his sister had been a neat move. But soon he turned against the king and, supported by other disaffected Earls, assembled a significant army that took control of the country by defeating the royal forces led by Henry's son, Prince Edward, at the battle of Lewis. The prince was taken prisoner. Simon de Montfort began running the country in the king's name.

He is credited with being the first in the world to create a kind of parliament. He twice summoned representatives of towns and shires to discuss issues of concern. It was hardly democracy in the modern sense, with knights, earls, clergy and burgesses selected for the 'parliaments'. But it was a radical departure from royal decree. Less known is de Montford's ruthless persecution of Jews, expelling them or massacring them in many towns and cities across England. He met his own doom at Evesham after many barons had deserted his cause. Prince Edward (later King Edward I) had been helped to escape, and assembled a mighty fighting force.

On August 4th, 1265, there was a heavy thunderstorm over Worcestershire as Simon de Montford's army marched north from the Abbey towards Greenhill, the higher ground where Prince Edward had lined up his troops. Shakespeare sometimes used descriptions of the weather to indicate dramatic developments about to unfold. This crashing thunder was no theatrical sound-effect, and may have unnerved the rebel army. More unnerving would have been the sight of ten thousand troops on the ridge. Simon de Montford's army numbered only about five thousand, and the expected reinforcements led by his son couldn't get across the Avon because the royalist forces held the bridge. The battle soon became a massacre. The contemporary historian Robert of Gloucester called it, "the murder of Evesham, for battle it was none." De Montford was killed and his body chopped to pieces which were sent to various parts of the kingdom as a deterrent to any other earls who may have been inclined to challenge the king.

Historians say the Battle of Evesham was a decisive moment in British history – the beginning of the end of the barons' opposition to Henry III and ushering in a period of stable monarchy. There is a waymarked trail around the site of the battle on Greenhill, with information boards about the 1265 battle. This was not the last time the waters of the Avon would run red here. During the English Civil War, Evesham was a royalist garrison. In 1645 a parliamentary force of cavalry and foot soldiers led by Colonel Edward Massey from Gloucester charged down the very same Greenhill and overwhelmed the royalists trapped in the loop of the river. Evesham remained in parliamentary hands until the end of the Civil Wars.

The Floods of 2007

Evesham has been particularly vulnerable to flooding for centuries. There are records from the thirteenth century of the river overflowing its banks. But the floods of July 2007 were the worst the town has ever experienced. Torrential rain – more than 3 times the average for the time of year – saw the Avon surge to 5 metres (16 feet) above its normal level. 330 properties were flooded and tethered narrowboats sank. Children were trapped in their schools, hotel guests were stuck on the top floors, and the District Council set up emergency centres in Evesham and Pershore for families flooded out of their homes.

Since then the Environment Agency has built a 600 metre long barrier of metal embedded in clay along part of the left bank to protect the most vulnerable houses, and near Broadway to the south there is a new water storage area which should syphon off rising waters that in the past have flooded villages across the vale. But the Environment Agency has been underfunded for years, and struggles to provide enough flood defences as extreme weather events happen more frequently, threatening properties both inland and around the coasts. And local authorities have experienced budget cuts for a decade. So in Evesham many people have taken matters into their own hands.

Residents of riverside houses each paid £12,000 for a flood barrier. Interviewed by the BBC, Guy Stevenson, who owns one of the houses said, "It is a large amount of investment but it puts everyone's minds at rest - there has to be a massive amount of water before it comes over." I reckon peace of mind is well worth the cost. And there are some new developments designed by architects with the threat of flooding in mind. A row of riverside apartments has been built on tall stone pillars. Enter up a flight of steps and your ground floor is well above historic flooding levels. This design of houses on platforms or stilts might become the norm in areas prone to flooding.

Red Lane to Some Perfect Villages

The track leading west from Evesham leaves the riverside for about 3 miles and goes up an incline into open countryside with excellent views of the town to the right, and beyond to the hill where the famous battle was fought. The track is called Red Lane, and certainly the hedgerows are loaded with dark red hawthorn berries and scarlet holly and rose hips. I can hear plenty of rustling in the bushes and the unmistakable 'chack-chack-chack' of fieldfares. These large and colourful thrushes have just arrived from their breeding grounds in northern Europe, and with the smaller redwings are wasting no time in stripping the hedges of their bounty of haws, holly berries and sloes.

About a fifth of the world's 11,000 bird species migrate, some huge distances, some shorter hops. The winter thrushes that descend on the British Isles are escaping the iron-hard weather in northern Scandinavia, Eastern Europe and Russia. The Woodland Trust reckons that about 600,000 fieldfares arrive here each autumn. Their name came from the Anglo-Saxon 'fildware', meaning the traveller of the fields. I've seen a flock of migrating fieldfares with each one carrying a berry in its beak; clearly having eaten their fill on arrival at the coast, they take a bit of packed lunch with them to swallow when they start getting peckish on the next leg inland.

Our path goes through the village of Charlton with its picturesque village green and a stream called 'Merrybrook' running through the middle. The Gardeners Arms invites me to linger awhile, but I press on past the neighbouring village of Cropthorne towards Fladbury. All the villages around here are picture-postcard pretty. About half of Cropthorne is designated as a conservation area, with plenty of half-timbered cottages, orchards stretching down to the riverbank and views to the Malvern Hills. The path rejoins the Avon with Jubilee Bridge taking us to the north bank. The jubilee in question was Queen Victoria's Golden Jubilee in 1887, commemorating 50 years on the throne. But the bridge didn't quite make its own jubilee. It had to be replaced in 1935 with three long, low steel arches.

On the other side of the bridge is the ancient village of Fladbury. There's a rushing weir with a red brick water mill at either side of a wide mill pool, and a lock to allow narrowboats to be lifted past the weir. It's a beautiful spot. The American artist John Singer Sargent, visited Fladbury in 1889. His painting, 'Two Girls with Parasols at Fladbury', is in the Metropolitan Museum of Art in New York.

Fladbury is mentioned in the 11th century Domesday Book, but there has been a riverside settlement here well before that. Excavations in the nineteen thirties revealed evidence of a Beaker community in the centre of Fladbury. The Beaker People lived in northern Europe in the late neolithic and early bronze age periods – that's 4,500 years ago. Their communities are named after the distinctive drinking cups finely decorated with zig-zag lines. They were probably nomadic hunters, but very little is known about the people who left their beakers behind to be unearthed thousands of years later.

Wyre Piddle

With the Avon looping away to the left, the path leaves the outskirts of Fladbury across farmland, through a holiday park clustered around some attractive lakes, past greenhouses and barns and on through some scrubland with chattering magpies on the tops of the thorn bushes. The way then joins the road into Wyre Piddle. Below a steep bank to the left, parallel with the main street, runs the River Avon, with woodland on the far bank, yellow and gold in the thin sunshine. Unlike its neighbouring villages upstream, Wyre Piddle on its high bank is in little danger from the floods that are happening more frequently in these parts. If the Avon overflows its banks here, the water will pour into the woods on the opposite side.

There is an ancient cross at the entrance to the village, with any writing or date eroded by time. It may have been standing there in 1471 when the Wars of the Roses were reaching their bloody climax. Perhaps at that time a wealthy landowner, fearful of King Edward VI's army heading for Tewkesbury, buried his cache of silver coins and never had the chance to recover them. In 1967, the hoard was discovered – 219 silver coins, some from early as 1280 and none later than 1467.

Overlooking the river is the seventeenth century Anchor Inn. It has a sign directing visitors round the side to 'Wyre Piddle Beach'. I duck inside and speak to the landlady who has recently taken over the pub. I ask about the beach. "Oh yes. The previous owners decided to create a beach at the bottom of the slope so that people could sunbathe and swim in the river. But the dogs and cats liked it too much", she explained, "so the customers weren't too keen to sunbathe there! We've replaced it with decking, which is more popular." I'm not surprised.

As she is speaking, a narrowboat is mooring at the deck, with a party of four stopping for a pint or lunch. There are tables on various levels of decking overlooking the slow-moving river and the golden woods. The weather is still mild enough for sitting outside in this sheltered spot. The Anchor used to serve locally brewed beers called 'Piddle in the Hole' and 'Piddle in the Wind' before the Wyre Brewery was dissolved in 2015. That's a shame! I would have quite enjoyed leaning on the bar and saying casually, "I'd like a piddle in the hole, please." The path out of the village passes the site of the old brewery near a concrete bridge that takes us over Piddle Brook, a tributary of the Avon that gave the village its name. Ahead there are good views of Pershore Abbey a mile away. Before long there are sports fields, and several large car parks, testament to Pershore's appeal to thousands of visitors each year.

November

Pershore to Eckington Bridge

We have some salt of our youth in us.
(Justice Shallow, Act II Scene 3, The Merry Wives
of Windsor)

Barn Owl

Plum Capital

There has been a settlement on the banks of the Avon at Pershore since the Iron Age – that's about 3,000 years ago - and there's archeological evidence of Roman occupation. After the destruction of Twyford Bridge a mile upstream during the Civil War, Pershore was on the main trade route between London and Worcester, and it flourished in the 18th century as its fruit and vegetables became more in demand from the growing populations in the industrial midlands. But in about 1750 a new road was constructed connecting Evesham and the old Worcester road, and the route through Pershore became less important.

It's recorded that in the 11th century, Edward the Confessor removed many of the possessions of Pershore Abbey, and bestowed them on an abbey he had refounded at Westminster. According to historians Page and Willis-Bund, "King Edward's gift included various liberties, sac and soc, toll and team, infangenthef, forstal, miskening and other privileges"(!), and gave the local abbot the right to establish a borough at Pershore, with a new parish church, St. Andrew's. The borough covered half of the town, in effect dividing it into two parishes, with an Abbot of Westminster on one side and the Abbot of Pershore on the other.

The town is known for its Georgian architecture, with scores of listed buildings along the High Street, Bridge Street and Broad Street, with elegant symmetry and classical architectural references. The Pershore Heritage Centre inside the Town Hall has impressive displays of artefacts and old documents chronicling Pershore's rich history. This thriving town is worth a visit at any time of year, with independent shops dotted along the High Street, and scores of pubs and restaurants.

It is a Market Town, which means it received a royal charter permitting a weekly market, which became famous in the region for its fruit and veg in season, notably plums. Pershore is the proud plum capital of Britain. In August there is a Plum Festival with plum-themed art and the crowning of a plum princess. It has given the world varieties such as the Pershore Yellow Egg Plum, Pershore Purple and Pershore Emblem. And just in case you hadn't got the idea, in the High Street there is The Pickled Plum – an old pub that you could say is well preserved. The market itself is housed in a splendid brick hall and these days offers more than fruit and veg, from haberdashery to hairstyling.

An Ancient Abbey and a Short-lived Bird

Just across the road stands the Abbey, or what remains of it – the abbey church. Founded in the year 689 by King Oswald, most of the architecture visible now is from the medieval period. The great Benedictine monastery, one of the largest in England, was substantially destroyed by Henry VIII's commissioners. But 'The Abbey Church of the Holy Cross' remains as a parish church. It's impressive. The Abbey Church is made of a local yellow stone that glows pink or orange in sunlight, though a large darker patch is apparently scorching from the fire that badly damaged the abbey in the eleventh century.

Inside, the soaring nave and aisles are famous for their 13th century ploughshare vaulting, so called because the shape of the stonework between the supporting ribs resemble the blade of a medieval plough. I crane my neck and marvel at the workmanship achieved without modern power tools. The original vaulting is still solidly supporting the roof and the great tower after more than 800 years.

The abbey stands in an extensive park with close-cut grass and impressive ancient trees – cedars, oaks and Scots pines. Walking beneath their huge branches I can hear a very high-pitched tinkling call. And just above my head, almost within touching distance are two goldcrests. They frequently hover under the branches to find spiders or aphids under the leaves, so I can see that one is an adult with the bright yellow stripe on its crown; the other is a juvenile with much paler markings. The smallest bird in Britain, weighing just 6 grams - the same as a 2p coin - the goldcrest is very 'confiding'. That's the birdwatchers' word meaning it ignores the presence of humans and can be observed at close range. But the tiny goldcrests can easily be overlooked, especially since many people can't hear them. Their reeling song and siii-siii calls are at such a high register that, as we get older, we can't pick up the sounds. I am fortunate in that my hearing is still pretty good. But if you are over sixty, the song of the goldcrest may be a frequency too far.

These two in the Abbey Park may be residents, or new arrivals from afar. Astonishingly, thousands of these tiny birds migrate here from Scandinavia in the autumn. Ringing has shown that some have come from as far away as Poland and Russia, and a few have made the return journey in the spring. They are unlikely to make the journey more than once. Many young birds don't make it to maturity, and 80% of adults perish each year, usually from cold in the winter; so the average life expectancy of a goldcrest is only about 8 months, the shortest for any British bird.

Parasitic Mistletoe

On the other side of the river from the Abbey Park, a line of tall poplars is adorned with huge spheres of mistletoe. Perhaps plagued would be a better word, for mistletoe is a clever parasite that can kill off the crown of its host tree by intercepting the moisture and nutrients feeding the leaves. Most mistletoe seeds are spread by birds that eat the white berries; the seeds come out in the droppings, or more frequently they are wiped on to a branch as the bird cleans its bill, because the seeds are covered in a very sticky material called viscin.

When the viscin is wiped on to a stem it sticks tenaciously, then hardens. The seed germinates inside this protective coating and and its tiny roots penetrate the bark. The berries are a favourite of the mistle thrush, hence its name. But the berries are poisonous to humans. The European species of mistletoe is particularly toxic, and can make you suffer from a number of serious illnesses, sometimes even causing cardiac arrest. So don't make tea from mistletoe leaves!

In pagan mythologies around the world, the white mistletoe berries have been seen as symbols of male fertility with the viscous seeds resembling semen. The Ancient Greeks referred to mistletoe as 'oak sperm' and the Celts regarded mistletoe as the semen of Taranis, the god of thunder. The Romans associated mistletoe with peace and love, and hung it over doorways during their winter Saturnalia celebrations; so in the Christian era the two traditional ideas seem to have blended into the notion that a woman standing under the mistletoe at Christmas time can't refuse a kiss. In Pershore there's no shortage of mistletoe to hang over doorways next month.

Another Historic Bridge

Leaving the High Street and the Abbey behind, Shakespeare's Avon Way goes through a residential area to Old Pershore Bridge. To my mind this is one of the most attractive bridges across the Avon. Records show that a bridge was built here in 1413 by monks, supposedly after their abbot was unfortunately drowned after slipping from stepping stones. There's a nineteenth century picture of the scene in one of the abbey windows. The old bridge has been damaged and repaired several times, notably after some violent skirmishes during the English Civil War in 1644.

Local historian Mike Pryce says that Charles I ordered the bridge to be destroyed to foil the pursuing Parliamentarians. Teams of soldiers and 'countrymen' set about the task with such vigour that part of the bridge collapsed with dozens of men still on it or working under it. Three dozen men were reportedly drowned, including the officer in charge who happened to be called Major Bridge. It's said the marks and scars on the bridge parapet date back to the Civil War battles to control the crossing point.

The repaired Pershore Bridge constructed of limestone is plain and simple and and pleasing to the eye, with a main rounded archway big enough for narrow boats and launches, and smaller arches on either side in the same rounded shape. In the warmer weather it's a great spot for a picnic. Next to the bridge is 'The Pershore Bridges Picnic Place', maintained by the County Council with moorings, an anglers' platform, information boards and toilets. It's called 'Bridges' because as well as the old bridge there is a new one in view. Well, not so new now. The old bridge used to carry the Evesham road, but in the nineteen twenties, as motor traffic increased, a new bridge was built nearby and the old bridge is now for walkers only. The floods that afflict this area have threatened to overwhelm the Old Pershore Bridge several times, with racing water almost reaching the top of the arches. But the sturdy old bridge has stood firm.

As we leave the abbey town behind, the river loops away to the right, and Shakespeare's Avon Way goes through housing developments, past playing fields and allotments until it rejoins the riverbank just before Comberton Quay where in days gone by grain was loaded on to barges to be taken to Nafford Mill.

Now it's a popular overnight mooring place for narrowboaters. The path leads away from the river up a sharp incline to the village of Old Comberton, founded in Anglo Saxon times on a shoulder of Bredon Hill, so it is safe from the regular floods in the Avon valley. The village has an attractive church dedicated to St. Michael and All Angels, and is popular with walkers who are heading for the summit of Bredon Hill. It also has a red telephone box.

The K6

The phone box has been converted into a local lending library. I really like this idea. A book exchange has been going on here for several years, all based on trust. Drop off a book you have read, and pick up another. In recent years, these telephone boxes have become as British as the changing of the guard. There's one in my home town of Warwick, and it often has tourists from the United States and the Far East posing as though on the phone to De Moines or Tokyo. To be technical they are examples of the K6 box, which stands for Kiosk Number 6.

The K6 with its embossed crown over the door and heavy cast iron frame was designed by Sir Giles Gilbert Scott to commemorate the Silver Jubilee of the coronation of George V in 1935 at a time when the telephone network was expanding across the country, but only the well-to-do could afford their own line. About 60,000 Scott K6 boxes were installed across Britain, of which about 11,000 remain, many with different functions. Some contain defibrillators, a few are mini greenhouses, and some have turned into village lending libraries. The K6 even has its own website and groups of K6 enthusiasts try to catalogue every one in the country. I think Sir Giles would have been proud.

Bredon Hill

It's about a mile up a very steep path from Old Comberton to the top of Bredon Hill. The view is worth the climb. On a clear, crisp November day you can see eight counties. The flat top is the remains of an iron age fort called Kemerton Camp. Historians reckon it was abandoned in the first century shortly after the Romans invaded Britain, following a considerable battle between the Celts and the Roman military. There are several ancient standing stones on the hill. One large rock at the summit is called the Banbury Stone or locally the 'Elephant Stone' because, well, from a certain angle it looks like an elephant! Another pair of stones below the summit is known as the King and Queen. Local legend tells that if you pass between them you will be cured of any illness.

The main feature on the summit is a stone tower called 'Parson's Folly', built in the 18th century as a summer house by John Parsons MP, the squire of nearby Kemerton Court. The hill is 981 feet high, and the squire was keen to reach the 1,000 foot mark with his summer house, so it was built 19 feet high, achieving the thousand feet in total.

Bredon Hill has been featured in the work of many composers, poets, authors and artists, including Poem 21 in A. E. Housman's anthology, 'A Shropshire Lad.'

> Here of a Sunday morning
> My love and I would lie,
> And see the coloured counties,
> And hear the larks so high
> About us in the sky.

Certainly in the spring it's known for its skylarks. Bredon Hill is an important wildlife site, with a range of unusual habitats including calcareous (alkaline) grassland, scrub and ancient woodland. A large part of the hillside is a Site of Special Scientific Interest (SSSI) and another area has been designated as a National Nature Reserve. On a chilly November day, there are no skylarks singing, but there are some about if you look carefully.

There is a large sloping field of stubble bordered by a dry stone wall, and several pale, mottled larks are picking their way along the furrows, brilliantly camouflaged. And I can hear there must be a stonechat around. This dumpy little bird, slightly smaller than a robin, gets its name from its alarm call, which resembles the sound of two stones being struck together. It pops up on to the wall – a male, showing his rusty chest, black face and white collar. Some stonechats head for the Mediterranean region in the winter, but most stay in the UK, especially since our winters in the southern half of Britain have become less harsh in recent years.

The descent back down to the Avon Way is somewhat easier than the climb to the top, and there is a pleasant walk across fields to Nafford with views of the Malvern Hills in the distance. These bare hills make me think of a children's story when a dragon, or a dinosaur, rises up out of the ground after being disturbed from its deep sleep. The Malverns are thought to be about 680 million years old and are very hard volcanic rocks thrown up through a fault. The name comes from the Celtic 'moel-bryn' meaning bare hill, with the nearest modern equivalent the Welsh 'moelfryn'. The water that emerges at the foot of the Malverns is extraordinarily pure H2O with no mineral impurities. For many years it has enjoyed the royal seal of approval. Queen Victoria would never travel to her dominions without a supply of Malvern Water, and it is reported that Elizabeth II always had a case or two in the royal luggage on her travels.

Gwen's Legacy

The River Avon is now a substantial waterway and the sound of rushing water ahead tells walkers they have reached Nafford Weir and Lock. A metal footbridge takes the path above the weir to the north bank where it skirts a nature reserve with a string of small lakes. This is the Gwen Finch Wetland, named after a resident of nearby Birlingham. She loved otters and had been thrilled to see them in the Avon in the 1980s when they were extremely rare in England. When she died in 1996, Gwen left £40,000 in her will for a project to encourage otters to thrive. With the aid of the legacy, the Worcestershire Wildlife Trust bought this marshy area and developed a diverse habitat of pools, scrapes, reed beds and water meadows.

Now otters are seen here regularly, along with bird species that are declining elsewhere because of the loss of wet habitats, such as lapwings, redshanks and reed warblers. The reserve isn't open to the public, but with binoculars it's easy to see the pools and scrapes from the path. There are mallard, gadwall and teal in spanking new breeding plumage, and herons fluffed up against the cold. Perhaps Gwen might inspire some of us to add to our wills a small legacy to develop wild habitats in our own areas.

Ghost Bird

The month is ending with Storm Arwen sweeping through the north-west of England. The high winds and heavy rain miss the Midlands, but shreds of purple clouds to the west provide some striking sunsets. A pure white little egret flies across heading for its roost, but illuminated from below by the setting sun, it looks as pink as a flamingo. And across the reserve towards a kink in the river known as The Swan's Neck, another pale bird is just visible in the evening light, flying low, to and fro, across a patch of reed bed. It is number 97 on my Avon bird list. The beautiful barn owl is the most widespread of the owl family, found all over the world apart from polar or desert regions. But in Britain their numbers dropped dramatically after the war as intensive farming practices removed the rough ground favoured by their staple food, voles and mice.

The British Trust for Ornithology estimates that in the fifty years to the mid-1980s, the number of breeding pairs had fallen by 70% to about 4,500. But now they have made a remarkable comeback, thanks to human intervention. The ecologist and writer, Colin Shawyer, can take a lot of the credit. In 1988 he established the Barn Owl Conservation Trust, campaigning for patches of agricultural land to be left fallow. He soon realised that the decline in barn owl numbers wasn't just because of the loss of habitat. There was a shortage of nest sites; modern farm building weren't owl-friendly and many old hollow trees had been felled. His Conservation Trust supplied owl boxes to farmers and landowners across the country. More than 20,000 have been erected so far. Colin put up 4,000 himself! It worked. The number of breeding pairs is now up to about twelve thousand. But being mainly nocturnal, these attractive birds remain difficult to see.

Barn owls have fantastic hearing. The heart-shaped facial disc acts as a sound-receiver, and with one ear placed slightly further back than the other, it can judge distance as well as direction even in pitch darkness. They remain silent much of the time and their very soft feathers allow them to fly noiselessly. In the breeding season, and at the nest site, they may issue a rather blood curdling shriek or loud hiss. Traditional country names for the barn own include 'shriek owl', 'ghost owl' and 'church owl'. The shriek of the white owl in the churchyard was, for many, a portent of death. I prefer the ancient folklore in the Far East that associates owls with wisdom.

December

Eckington Bridge to Tewkesbury

How like a winter hath my absence been
From thee, the pleasure of the fleeting year!
What freezings have I felt, what dark days seen!
What old December's bareness every where!
(Shakespeare's Sonnet 97)

Egyptian Geese

The Red Stone Bridge

A short cold spell ushers in December, with sharp frost in the mornings, and the occasional snow flurry with the flakes melting almost as soon as they hit the ground. Snowflakes have fascinated meteorologists and physicists for hundreds of years, since Zacharias Janssen, the son of a Dutch spectacle-maker, invented the first microscope in 1590, at the same time as Shakespeare was penning Two Gentlemen of Verona, Edward III, and The Taming of The Shrew that puts man-woman relationships under the microscope. How do snowflakes form? And is every one really different?

It's now known that a snowflake starts its brief life high in the atmosphere when a tiny speck of pollen or desert dust comes into contact with water vapour. It freezes into a minute crystal of ice. Because each water molecule has two hydrogen atoms and one oxygen atom, ($H2O$), the most efficient way for them to bind together to form a snowflake is for each crystal to grow with six symmetrical arms. I find it extraordinary that no two snowflakes are the same. The concept of an infinite number of hexagonal crystals is too difficult to grasp – rather like the notion of infinite space containing an infinite number of stars.

Soon the mild weather returns with thin cloud and light winds. Our path crosses to the left bank of the Avon at Eckington Bridge, where there is a picnic site beside the river, with the water eighty meters across in places and flowing strongly. The bridge itself is a scheduled ancient monument. It was built in the 1720s from the local rich-red sandstone, replacing a medieval bridge that had become unsafe. Now it carries the Pershore to Tewkesbury road, with lights controlling single-file traffic over the ancient structure. From the bridge, there's a view of the Malvern Hills straight ahead downstream, and Bredon Hill is visible upstream, but the traffic on the narrow bridge makes it difficult to linger. I doubt whether Arthur Quiller-Couch had that problem when he wrote 'Upon Eckington Bridge, River Avon', shortly after the First World War.

In the poem, written under his pseudonym 'Q', he reflects on the bloody battles that have taken place on the banks of the Avon over the centuries, and advocates the pastoral life of honest toil that he believes will outlast any war. His inspiration came from grooves in the stone bridge made by bargemen's ropes over countless years.

> *Man shall outlast his battles. They have swept*
> *Avon from Naseby Field to Savern Ham;*
> *And Evesham's dedicated stones have stepp'd*
> *Down to the dust with Montfort's oriflamme.[Blood-red*
> *banner]*
> *Nor the red tear nor the reflected tower*
> *Abides; but yet these elegant grooves remain,*
> *Worn in the sandstone parapet hour by hour*
> *By labouring bargemen where they shifted ropes;*
> *E'en so shall men turn back from violent hopes*
> *To Adam's cheer, and toil with spade again.*

Traveller's Joy

From Eckington Bridge it's a pleasant two mile walk beside the chuckling river to Strensham Lock, with farmland on either side and high hedges now stripped of their berries by the flocks of winter thrushes. The hedgerows are covered in great wispy white mounds of 'Traveller's Joy', *clematis vitalba,* with the feathery seeds blowing across the river and sprinkling the surface. It's also known widely as 'Old Man's Beard', or in some parts 'Bush Beards', 'Grandfather's Whiskers' and 'Withywine'. This rampant climber is native to southern Britain but in recent years, as our climate warms, it has been moving north as far as the Scottish border and is viewed by many as an unwelcome invasive species, overwhelming hedges and trees and stifling the growth of other plants.

But it has many good points too. In the summer it has a sweet scent and is an important source of nectar for bees, hoverflies, and moths. The Woodland Trust website reminds us that Traveller's Joy has been used in various traditional treatments as it's said to contain anti-inflammatory properties. The plant was often used to treat skin irritations and to relieve stress. Exactly how one should take the stress-medicine isn't explained. And in the past the woody stems were used to make baskets. The Woodland Trust says it's called Traveller's Joy because it adorns hedges and banks in the countryside with billows of beautiful feathery seed heads in the grey months leading up to Christmas. I certainly think this energetic clematis throwing white wisps into the air is quite joyful on a cold, grey day.

Uncommon birds

My count of different bird species during this year beside the Avon is going quite well. In the far distance I hear the trembling call of a curlew, a sound always associated in my mind with wild open spaces – high moors or low estuaries. Number 98. And much closer to hand in a clump of alders there is a sharp call – a very high pitched 'zee zee', followed by a more rasping 'chay-chay-chay'. Two willow tits are working their way along the river bank. These smart little birds with buff plumage, sooty black crowns and small black bibs have become rare in recent years.

The British Trust for Ornithology (BTO) reports that the number of breeding willow tits in Britain declined by 83%

between 1995 and 2017. This rapid collapse in numbers is believed be due to three factors. First, habitat loss. Willow tits are pretty choosy about where they live and breed, preferring old wet woodlands, a habitat largely removed by landowners because it has no commercial value. Secondly, competition for nest holes with other tits, particularly blue tits. As soon as a willow tit has pecked out a nest hole in a rotting tree, the prolific blue tits and great tits will bully it out and take over.

Thirdly, willow tits have suffered badly from nest predation by great spotted woodpeckers that will hammer their way into a nest hole and eat the eggs or young. For various reasons, including the huge increase in the number of people putting out garden feeders containing peanuts, during the same period that the BTO was tracking the decline of the willow tit, the woodpecker numbers increased fourfold. So it is fabulous to find a pair of these beautiful little rare birds along the riverbank. They are number 99 on the year-long journey.

Feeding the Birds

So should we feed the birds? By doing so, are we interfering with the natural cycle? Putting out bird food in the winter has become a widespread habit in Britain. Bird seed costs more than tuppence a bag these days. According to the British Trust for Ornithology, 17 million households spend £250 million each year on choice peanuts, niger seed, mealworms, fat balls, and 'premium mixed wild bird seed'. A recent research paper from Manchester Metropolitan University posed the question of whether this might do more harm than good.

Professor Alex Lees says there are two problems. First, the bolder garden bird species such as blue tits flourish at the expense of more timid species. He mentions the way willow tits and pied flycatchers are being bullied out of their nest holes by growing numbers of blue tits and great tits, and the increase in numbers of wood pigeons and goldfinches in urban areas, while the traditional town dwellers, sparrows and starlings, declined. The second problem is that feeders can spread disease. Mike Toms of the BTO says feeders should be thoroughly cleaned once a fortnight.

No one is suggesting that we all take down our feeders, but we can all keep them clean, and I suggest they are hung near some bushy cover wherever possible, so that the birds that are subservient to the dominant species have somewhere to lurk before they dash in for a snack. The university article confesses that more research is needed to establish whether or not feeding the birds disadvantages some species. But I for one will certainly keep putting out fat balls, peanuts and bird seed on cold winter days, and will enjoy watching the birds that eagerly come to feed on them. I am sure many more would die each winter without this ready source of energy-rich food.

Pronunciations

At Strensham Lock there are scores of boats, mainly small cruisers, sealed up for the winter and moored in a marina, part of which used to be a millpond. The lock with a swing bridge across it can take two narrowboats at a time passing the weir that used to power the old mill. The path leaves the riverbank for a couple of miles, crossing open fields and diving through a tunnel under the M5 before rejoining the Avon at Twyning.

The village name is pronounced 'Twinning'. The family of the tea merchants, Twinings, is said to have originated here in the Middle Ages, working as weavers, before they moved to London in 1684 and found success in the newly fashionable tea business. Confusingly, Twinings Tea is pronounced, 'Twynings'.

In those days The Fleet Inn at Twyning ('Twinning') had a ferry across the river. Henry VIII had awarded the landlord a licence to collect tolls. But the river is a substantial waterway here, and can run fast after heavy rains, and in the 1960s the ferry was considered too hazardous and was closed. There's a stiff breeze rippling the water as I look out, and hissing in the willows. Did you know there is a name for the sound of the wind in the trees? 'Psithurism' The p is silent – as in bathing, as my father used to joke about the p in Thompson. The word psithurism comes from the Ancient Greek word for whispering.

Tewkesbury

After visiting Worcestershire, the Warwickshire Avon has now quietly passed into Gloucestershire for the last leg of its journey. It is an easy riverside stroll into the north end of Tewkesbury. The river divides here with a narrow branch called the Mill Avon that powered an old mill serving the great Tewkesbury Monastery, and is the western boundary of the town. It creates a large island between the Mill Avon and the Severn called the Severn Ham, as mentioned in Quiller-Couch's poem. The old mills, warehouses and chandleries are now converted into desirable residences with views across the flood plain, but the tall brick buildings still speak of Tewkesbury's importance through the centuries as a trading hub, with access to the Atlantic sea routes, and to the Severn and Avon Navigations, bringing manufactured goods to be shipped around the world.

The town itself was a centre for leather-making and textiles. In medieval times there were scores of leather companies in Tewkesbury, with guilds representing tanners, glovers, hatters, saddlers and cordwainers (shoemakers). When the leather business began to wane, the enterprising burgers of Tewkesbury switched to textiles made from wool. Then, as imported cotton replaced wool, it became a cotton town specialising in stockings.

Illegal stockings and Golden Balls

In 1830 the hosiery business employed about 1,500 people in the town with 800 frames operating. They were able to undercut the prices of the cotton towns in the north and midlands because Tewkesbury stockings were made with less yarn. They used two yarns instead of three. But their stockings were less durable, and the established hosieries raised a stink about the cheap wares from Gloucestershire. In 1776, an Act of Parliament was passed, at the instigation of the City of Nottingham that was being driven into poverty by Tewkesbury's success. It made Tewkesbury's 'two-yarn stockings' illegal. They became known as 'Tewkesbury Frauds.'

But as well as producing cotton goods, Tewkesbury flourished from a number of other trades that attracted workers from the surrounding countryside, including pin-making, brewing and mustard making. In Henry IV Part II, Falstaff described Ned Poins as having 'a wit as thick as Tewkesbury Mustard.' I think he was suggesting Ned was a bit thick. The Tewkesbury Mustard Company still sells traditional mustard balls - dried versions of the hot condiment. In 2020 the company applied for Protected Geographical Indication (PGI) status for its mustard and mustard balls, which would have given them the same protected status as Cornish pasties and Melton Mowbray pork pies. 'Tewkesbury Mustard' would have to be produced in the area to an agreed recipe.

I don't think the application was successful, but in the town you can get some unique local specialities including mustard flavoured chocolate, and gold mustard balls. These are made with mustard-flour, cider and horseradish, and are coated in edible real gold leaf. Just £15 a ball. Apparently golden balls like these adorned the banqueting table of Tewkesbury Abbey when Henry VIII and his queen, Ann Boleyn, visited the town in 1535. The extravagant treats did not save the abbey from dissolution a few years later.

The Alleyways

As more and more people moved into town to find work in the flourishing craft industries, the place became packed. Confined by the Rivers Severn and Avon and their flood plains that were unsuitable for building, half-timbered houses were crammed into every available space in the town centre, with upper stories leaning out above narrow lanes. Known as The Alleyways, there used to be ninety of them zig-zagging between the tall houses. Thirty alleyways remain today. They link the main street to the riverside, and are a famous feature of this ancient town. Incidentally, the name Tewkesbury is thought to come from a seventh century Christian missionary called Theoc, (which would have been pronounced 'Teoc' in Old English). He founded a hermitage where the great abbey now stands and by the time of Domesday Book, the name Theocsbury had become Tewkesbury.

The Great Abbey

The magnificent Abbey Church of Mary the Virgin standing in parkland on the south side of town is a world-renowned example of early medieval religious architecture. It recently celebrated 900 years since it was consecrated. The Normans brought with them not only their preferred Romanesque style of church building with rounded arches, they also brought the stone. It is called Caen stone, a cream-coloured, durable limestone from a quarry near the city of Caen in northern France. Great slabs were ferried across the Channel and up the Severn to Tewkesbury, where skilled masons fashioned the long, soaring nave topped with a huge tower and supported by 18 massive round pillars.

The roof of the nave is noted for its decorative bosses; these were added in the 14th century when the church was extended. If you visit I recommend that you take your binoculars, as I did. Then you can see the details of the richly painted bosses, but you may risk a cricked neck. From the same period there are seven stained glass windows showing biblical figures, prophets and earls. They are said to be among the most outstanding survivors of 14th century glass in the whole of Europe. In these December days before Christmas, the church is decorated with a huge tree covered in gold baubles. I don't think they contain dried mustard.

The entire abbey church was fortunate to survive Henry VIII's dissolution of the monasteries when he declared himself head of the Church of England and seized the assets of the the religious houses across the country. The abbey was the centrepiece of a Benedictine monastery that was closed, then dismantled. The people of Tewkesbury argued that the abbey church was their parish church, and the King had ruled that parish churches should not be plundered or closed. But the townspeople were told they had to buy the place from the crown; the price? £453, the value of the metal from the bells and the lead from the roof. To this day, the great Abbey Church of Mary the Virgin remains as Tewkesbury's parish church, carefully maintained and hosting many community events.

Water water everywhere ...

In July 2007, the parishioners found themselves ankle deep in water, lifting valuable items to safety. Following a very dry April, the summer of 2007 was one of the wettest on record across the country with flooding in Scotland, Yorkshire and the Midlands. But Gloucestershire was particularly badly affected. On Friday 20th July, two months' worth of rain fell in 14 hours, resulting in two emergencies; widespread flooding and shortages of drinking water. The floodwater funnelling down the Severn and the Avon, inundating hundreds of riverside properties, and where the two rivers meet in Tewkesbury, the swollen waters surged over the banks flooding 1,800 homes and cutting off the town.

On Sunday 22nd July, Mythe Water Treatment works half a mile north of Tewkesbury was overwhelmed with polluted water and had to be shut down. This left 350,000 people across Gloucestershire without drinking water for up to seventeen days – the largest loss of essential services since the Second World War. Since then an eleven-foot-high wall has been built to protect the treatment plant. In the town itself a public consultation has been going on for years about plans drawn up by the Environment Agency to prevent a repeat of the 2007 disaster. It involves multiple flood walls and 'bunds' to contain or divert floodwaters, all costing an estimated £28 million. The residents clearly hope that the defences are completed before there's another huge flood. As climate change accelerates, that is becoming more likely in the coming years.

The Final Battle

To the south of the Abbey are some open fields and an area of raised ground where the long-running Wars of the Roses in the fifteenth century came to a bloody conclusion, with the River Avon playing its part once again. Margaret of Anjou at the age of fifteen had married Henry VI of England, a member of the Lancastrian dynasty. When the king began suffering from bouts of insanity, she in effect ruled in his place, gaining a formidable reputation as a tough and skilful negotiator who was determined that her son, Prince Edward, would inherit the crown. But her French origins and lavish lifestyle made her unpopular, and she became convinced that the powerful Richard Duke of York was plotting to seize the crown. According to Shakespeare, indeed he was! Henry was deposed and replaced by Richard's son, another Edward, who became King Edward IV. But Margaret would not relinquish her son's claim to the crown.

After a series of battles up and down the country between the Lancastrians and the Yorkists who were led by Edward IV, the two armies met just outside Tewkesbury on May 4th. 1471. The setting is the climax of Shakespeare's trilogy of Henry VI plays recounting the Wars of the Roses. Queen Margaret led the Lancastrian forces into battle personally, but they soon became trapped by the Severn and a small river, the Swilgate, curving behind their positions to join the Avon. It became a deadly barrier to the soldiers retreating from a hail of arrows and cannon fire. Many were drowned or killed by their pursuers. It was a disaster for the Lancastrian earls supporting Margaret and her son Prince Edward. He was executed on the battlefield. She was taken prisoner, to be ransomed and returned to France three years later. Many of the other nobles supporting her cause sought sanctuary in the Abbey. It didn't prove to be a sanctuary at all. After a brief standoff, the Yorkists dragged them out and killed them all. Dark marks on the flagstones are said to be stains from the streams of blood.

Shakespeare seemed to be fascinated by the character of Margaret. In Richard III, he has her return from France to the English court where she behaves as a Cassandra-like prophetess. She dramatically curses the majority of the nobles for their roles in the death of her son and the downfall of the House of Lancaster. All of her curses come to pass as the noblemen are betrayed and executed by Richard of Gloucester.

The Tewkesbury Battlefield Society hold monthly guided walks around 'The Bloody Meadow', the main site of the slaughter. And in July each year, the town stages a fabulous Medieval Festival with music, falconry, archery and jesters. It's the biggest event of its kind in Europe. The climax is a re-enactment of the 1471 Battle of Tewkesbury. Thousands take part in authentic period costumes, with swords clashing and cannons firing.

Unusual Geese – Not Geese

To find the confluence of the Avon and the Severn, I retrace my steps northwards along Church Street and the High Street, past the 15th Century Royal Hop Pole Hotel, reminding us of this region's brewing traditions. The street is festooned with strings of golden lights for Christmas. The footbridge across the river joins The Severn Way, the longest riverside path in Britain at more than 200 miles in length. And there it is, partly obscured by high grass and brambles - the confluence of the Severn and the Avon. The water is moving quite fast. The late afternoon sun is weak. There is a chilly breeze hissing the reeds. And on the opposite bank there are some strange-looking birds. They seem to be wearing dark glasses against the glare of the setting sun.

It is a pair of Egyptian Geese. To be precise, they are not geese, but ducks, related to our native shelducks. They have striking chestnut-brown, grey and white plumage, and bright pink legs. A common species in Africa, especially the Nile Valley, in recent years they have invaded Britain and their population here is exploding. Originally brought to adorn country estates in the 18th century, Egyptian Geese began breeding in the wild in East Anglia and are now spreading west and north. As an invasive species, they can be shot if causing trouble on farms. But so far there's no evidence of them damaging crops. They are grass-grazers.

Egyptian Geese nest very early. Indeed, at Christmas time this pair will have selected a rabbit hole or tree-hole already, and may hatch up to ten young as early as January. In the past this would have made the ducklings vulnerable to freezing weather and hungry predators, but the warmer weather of the last 20 years has clearly improved their survival rate. As a 'self-sustaining species', I can count them on my Avon wild bird list, and they become bird species number one hundred! Target accomplished. But they are not the only geese on this wide open flood plain.

I can hear some distant squawking up river, and narrowing my eyes against the yellowing light in the western sky, there are long v-shaped lines of geese approaching along the Severn. The skeins of birds must be half a mile across. Could they be Canada geese? No, they don't have black necks. Perhaps the chunkier greylags with their pale plumage? No. These geese are making squeakier sounds, very different from the braying and honking of the greylags. And they are a little smaller, and pale brown, with white showing under their tails.

A spectacular fly-by

These are pink-footed geese - at least two hundred of them, silhouetted against the shafts of evening sunlight. They have come a long way to overwinter in England. 'Pink-foots', as they are known by birdwatchers, breed in the far north tundra in Spitsbergen, Greenland and Iceland. They come to the British Isles to escape the harsh winters there. Most stop at estuaries in Ireland, Scotland and Northern England, but some venture further south. These skeins of geese may be heading for the Slimbridge wetland reserve further down the Bristol Channel.

I think they are brilliant birds, not only because they are number 101 on my Avon year list, but because they are so thoroughly wild while at the same time being communal. They avoid people and breed in collectives in the remote and harsh conditions to the north. They talk to each other on their long migrations, the adults protecting the younger birds and taking it in turns to blast at 40 mph into the headwinds at the front of the v-shaped formations. They have been making this journey each year for time beyond memory, perhaps since humans were living in caves. With the geese squeaking overhead, the hissing of the reeds below, and the low sun occasionally breaking through the clouds, it is easy to find oneself reflecting on fundamental things in a turbulent world, such as cherishing those that are close to you. But also valuing the eternal power of the natural world, a world that the nine billion humans on the planet must protect rather than plunder and destroy it.

Back home in Warwick, I find a daffodil in full bloom on January 31ˢᵗ in St. Nicholas' Churchyard, a few yards from the banks of the Avon. The Met Office reports that Britain has seen its warmest ever New Year's Eve. It was 15.8 degrees celsius in Somerset, a full degree warmer than the previous record in 2011 - a sign of things to come.

Reflections

The seasons alter: hoary-headed frosts
Fall in the fresh lap of the crimson rose,
And on old Hiems' thin and icy crown
An odorous chaplet of sweet summer buds
Is, as in mockery, set. The spring, the summer,
The childing autumn, angry winter, change
Their wonted liveries, and the mazed world,
By their increase, now knows not which is which.
(A Midsummer Night's Dream. Act 2.
Scene 1. Titania speaking.)

Pink-footed Geese

The Seasons Alter

Standing by the Avon on a crisp winter's day, the reflections in the water show a wobbly world turned upside down. In *A Midsummer Night's Dream*, the Forest of Arden that bordered the Avon was a refuge from mankind's dishonesties and cruelties. But even the healing power of nature was feeling the turbulence. Titania bemoans the altered seasons, when she can't tell which season is which in the 'mazed world'. It is almost as though Shakespeare, through his queen of the woodland fairies, is predicting climate disruption. And there is more than a suggestion of turbulence in society caused by human activity. As Hamlet expressed it, "Time is out of joint".

I had expected life would return to something more like normal following the worst of the pandemic years. Unfortunately the year that followed my walks along Shakespeare's Avon Way was to become a year of unfolding crises. The weather was certainly misbehaving. England sweltered in a summer heatwave and drought and the government's Health Security Agency issued the first ever 'national emergency heat red alert', urging people to stay out of the sun. The previous highest recorded temperature of 38.7 degrees celsius was smashed with 40.3 degrees recorded in Lincolnshire. Scores of fires in tinder-dry conditions had firefighters working round the clock to contain them. In Wennington, East London, a fire that broke out in gardens destroyed a row of houses.

Mainland Europe also suffered from extreme heat. Portugal registered 47 degrees. In Spain, Greece and France, wildfires forced thousands to flee their homes. According to the EU's Copernicus environmental programme, the summer drought in Europe was almost certainly the worst in 500 years. It was a similar story further afield, with a record 50.7 degrees in Western Australia triggering widespread bush fires, and in

California, huge forest fires covered San Francisco in choking smoke. Even Antarctica was affected, with record high temperatures causing some ice sheets to melt. This was not a freak one-off event. Copernicus calculated that globally the seven hottest years ever recorded were the previous seven years. And the trend seems to be accelerating.

Extreme heat was followed by other extreme weather events. Pakistan suffered huge floods following a record amount of monsoon rain and melt water from glaciers surging down the River Indus. A third of the country was underwater with millions made destitute. The United Nations Intergovernmental Panel on Climate Change, drawing on the work of thousands of scientists around the world, issued another stark report. The headline was, 'It's now or never if the world is to stave off climate disaster'. The report said greenhouse gas emissions must peak within three years to have a chance of keeping global heating at 1.5 degrees above pre-industrial levels. After that, certain tipping points would be reached with global heating accelerating. The UN Environment Programme followed up by saying there is 'no credible way' this can be achieved.

Rising temperatures – Rising prices

The drought in Europe had badly affected agriculture, notably in Spain and France. Food prices were rising. And there were other pressures on prices. According to the government's own analysis, global supply chains were under significant stress before the war in Ukraine. The UK's supply chain problems stemmed from worldwide shortages of key materials, staff shortages and transport delays. Most independent analysts say Brexit contributed to these problems with masses of extra paperwork, delays at Dover, and a shortage of lorry drivers. When Vladimir Putin's Russia brutally invaded Ukraine, the EU nations and NATO moved swiftly to help Ukraine repel the Russian westward advance. But at significant economic cost. With Russian oil and gas no longer flowing west, energy costs rocketed. UK inflation rapidly reached double-figures.

Public sector workers who had suffered a pay freeze for years were offered rises well below the inflation rate and began a series of strikes. After bailing out businesses during the Covid lockdowns, the government had to produce a support package for households and businesses facing unaffordable rises in energy bills. It cost many billions – money borrowed on the international markets, increasing the national debt to unprecedented levels.

Change at the Top

Within a 48-hour period Britain would have a new Prime Minister and a new Monarch – Charles III. As Prince of Wales he had been a prominent advocate for action to combat climate change and protect biodiversity. As the King, he may have to curb his personal views; it could prove difficult for him.

The new Prime Minister, Liz Truss, supported by right-wing members of the Conservative Party, made it clear straight away that she believed in unrestrained capitalism to produce economic growth that would solve the 'cost of living crisis' and make Britain a 'powerhouse'. Taxes would be cut, meaning more huge government borrowing and a squeeze on public expenditure. There was nothing new for the National Health Service, with its long waiting lists and shortages of staff, or care home staff, or child care provision, or environmental protection, or measures to combat climate change. The value of the pound fell, fuelling inflation.

"Wait a minute", I hear you say, "I thought this book would be about wildlife and history in the heart of England. This is politics!" Well, as Thomas Mann observed, "Everything is politics". Clearly that is true, and anyone who says, "Oh, I'm not interested in politics" is, in my view, misguided. How children are educated, the cost of living, the ability to rent or buy a home, success or failure in business, your health as you get older, public transport, even holes in the road – they are all political issues. And so is the environment. Before the Truss administration, the UK had committed to 'Net Zero' carbon emissions by 2050. In her first weeks in office she signalled that this would no longer be a priority. Nothing would stand in the way of business to achieve "growth, growth, growth."

Protecting our Environment

Most commentators agreed that any benefits from the go-for-growth policy would take some time to filter through. The UK had to become self-sufficient in energy as soon as possible. But instead of investing in a mass insulation programme, an energy saving campaign, and renewable sources such as wind and solar, the new government decided to issue about a hundred new licenses for oil and gas extraction in the North Sea, (which would take a decade to come on stream), lift the ban on fracking, (extracting gas from shale), and end the 'green levy' on our bills that helped to fund renewable energy development.

As for our valued natural environment and the need to reverse the loss of species, thirty-eight 'investment zones' would be created, with low business rates and relaxed planning rules making it easier to build industrial parks and housing on green land, including on protected sites. A bill introduced to parliament could lead to the removal of all EU environmental protections such as the Habitats Regulations. The big environmental groups were outraged.

The RSPB with 1.2 million members did not mince its words; "Make no mistake, we are angry. This government has launched an attack on nature. As of today, from Cornwall to Cumbria, Norfolk to Nottingham, wildlife is facing one of the greatest threats it's faced in decades." The chief executive of the Wildlife Trusts (870,000 members) called it "an unprecedented attack on nature launched by the UK government. We were previously reassured over nature protections lost through Brexit, but now nature is in catastrophe. We'll be challenging this together with other charities and asking for our supporters to stand with us." Even the National Trust, which probably has many Conservative voters among its 6 million members, pledged to work with other nature charities and supporters to 'defend important protections for nature long into the future.'

The Big Issue

The Liz Truss premiership that spooked the financial markets and horrified many people across the country did not last long. She was out after 44 days. But the large hole in the public finances was still gaping and needed to be plugged. How would the Rishi Sunak administration deal with the economic crisis? After years of austerity would there be another round of cuts to public spending? Would ministers continue to view environmental protection as an obstacle to growth? The ban on fracking was to remain – a small policy reversal but a welcome one. By the time you read this, there could be a more enlightened government in the UK that sees Climate Change as the greatest threat to future generations, and is prepared to raise money - yes, probably through taxes, - to invest in measures to cut our emissions of greenhouse gases by weaning us off fossil fuel generation, insulating our buildings, and protecting communities such as those along the banks of the Avon and the Severn. It is difficult to overstate the likely effects of continued global warming. Nearly everything will be affected by climate disruption.

For example the contentious subject of immigration. Many of the desperate people risking their lives to cross the channel in overcrowded rubber boats are fleeing war zones, but many others are fleeing climate change. The Horn of Africa is suffering a desperate drought. Who can blame the Somalis who trek across two contents to reach a more hopeful future? Of course immigration must be controlled. But 'send in the navy', or 'send them to Rwanda' surely can't be the solution, and it clearly hasn't worked as a deterrent. A warming climate will also bring more health challenges, and not just the hospitalisations during heatwaves. Scientists predict that malaria is likely to spread into northern Europe.

What Can I Do?

OK. It is a bleak picture. A walk in the country can lead us to reflect on the important things in our lives, and there's nothing more important than mankind despoiling our planet. But a riverside walk also tends to cheer us up. So let's be optimistic. If we all do a little bit to protect the planet, it will have an impact, and can have a cumulative effect as other people, and indeed other countries, sign up to the joint effort. What can we do?

Education

The first thing I would suggest is to spread the word. I guess that many people don't understand how critical the situation is becoming. Engage your friends and family in the conversation, and perhaps write to your MP asking him or her what they are doing to encourage emissions reduction and energy efficiency in their constituency and in parliament.

Education is key, especially when powerful vested interests in the oil and gas industry issue misleading information and deploy sophisticated lobbying. The decision to introduce a GCSE in Natural History from 2025 is a welcome development. The next generations will have to deal with the impacts of global warming. The Department of Education said, 'The new qualification will allow pupils to learn about organisms and their environments, and to understand sustainability issues. They will also do fieldwork to develop the skills needed to conserve wildlife, and to have the knowledge to be able to improve biodiversity and climate resilience.'

Support the Environmental Charities

Join up if you haven't done so already. For example, the county-based network of Wildlife Trusts does fantastic work managing habitats, protecting threatened species, advising landowners and educating young people. The Warwickshire Wildlife Trust in my area now manages 65 reserves. The Trust recently launched its 2030 Strategy with specific targets, including the aim of having 30% of land 'in recovery', and doubling the amount of habitat it directly manages. https://www.wildlifetrusts.org/

The RSPB owns no fewer than 222 reserves across the UK, and is an influential voice for nature conservation. For a few years I was a member of the RSPB governing council, when the charity was approaching a million members. Among other things, the council would approve land purchases based on priority habitats – ranging from wetlands, heathland

and coastal cliffs, to ancient forest and reclaimed industrial land where birds could be shown to urban communities. When an area of threatened habitat was put up for sale, and might be used for development, it was satisfying to be able to say, "Let's buy it and turn it into reserve". The growing number of membership fees made this possible. https://www.rspb.org.uk/

I am particularly impressed by the work of the Canal and River Trust. It was formed in 2012 when David Cameron's government was winding up some publicly owned bodies and transferring them to charitable trusts under the 'Big Society' banner. In England and Wales, the British Waterways Board ceased to exist, with the Trust taking over management of 2,000 miles of rivers and canals and the country's reservoirs. With the help of hundreds of volunteers, the Trust is cleaning up our waterways, restoring habitats, and is an effective voice in pressurising the privatised water companies to stop dumping raw sewage into our rivers. You can support their work by becoming a 'Friend' for £5 a month. https://canalrivertrust.org.uk/

The Woodland Trust protects our woods and forests which are carbon sinks as well as being wonderful wildlife habitat and great for restorative walks. https://www.woodlandtrust.org.uk/ Of course there are many more organisations involved in conservation in Britain. The National Trust manages large tracts of land as well as historic buildings. And the Bat Conservation Trust is the only national charity devoted to protecting these fascinating flying mammals.

You may even want to do some volunteer work to support your chosen local charity. But even if you can't do that, as a member you'll get excellent magazines that keep you informed about developments in nature protection and carry articles to help identification of wildlife. The more you know about the natural world, the more you are determined to protect it.

Use your vote wisely

Then there's always the politics. When it is time to vote in a local authority election, or in a general election, I would hope that habitat destruction, pollution, and above all Climate Change will be in more people's minds and will influence their decisions. We are a tribal species and many people tend to vote for the same party again and again almost automatically. But that is hardly a healthy democracy in action. We should study the environmental commitments of the candidates and parties and vote accordingly. We should judge a government by its actions not its rhetoric. As Shakespeare expressed it in King Henry VIII, 'Talking isn't doing. It is a kind of good deed to say well; and yet words are not deeds'.

At the local level there are positive signs that cities and towns now have embraced the importance of green spaces for the physical and mental health of residents. In Stockton on Tees, the 1970s Castlegate Shopping Centre is being demolished to be replaced with a five acre riverside park. Manchester has revised its plan for the regeneration of the Mayfield Development, involving 1,500 homes, offices, and shops, to include a large park with wild areas and water meadows as well as play areas. Sheffield is proposing a city centre public park on a site originally earmarked for a multi-storey car park. Southampton's plan for the redevelopment of its Bargate Shopping Area includes a 'linear park' alongside the old city walls.

Reduce our Carbon Footprints

There are many ways each of us can contribute to the overall reduction in damaging emissions. They include using less electricity in the home and at work, which also saves money. Insulating the home helps reduce energy consumption and the cost pays off in the long term. If we all used our cars a little less it would make a material difference, and would also improve air quality. Even saving water helps to reduce your carbon footprint. Maximum recycling means a reduction in the use of the world's resources; extracting raw materials has a carbon penalty. Eating more veg and less meat would help reduce emissions, and dietitians say it would be good for one's health. Paul McCartney's 'Meat Free Mondays' might be worth a thought. There are countless websites and online campaigns about personal carbon footprints with suggestions on ways we can make lifestyle choices that don't turn us all into miserable ascetics.

War – What is it good for?

Here's a final reflection. Shakespeare's Avon Way began at Naseby where thousands of yeomen, farmworkers and tradesmen were hacked to death alongside the professional soldiers. It ends at Tewkesbury, where once again the waters turned red with blood, with other battle sites along the way. England's history is a succession of terrible conflicts caused by the pursuit of power and wealth, or religious fanaticism. As I write, the war between Russia and Ukraine is making nuclear escalation a realistic possibility for the first time since the Cuban Missile Crisis in 1962, according to the President of the US. Extreme nationalism is irrational and dangerous. It must be condemned by all reasonable folks, and certainly rejected at the ballot-box.

As the optimistic Quiller-Couch observed as he stood on Eckington Bridge over the Avon, *Man shall outlast his battles.* In Shakespeare's Richard II, John of Gaunt knowing he would soon die from illness, casts himself as a 'prophet new inspired'. Bemoaning the violent divisions and mismanagement afflicting the country, he famously describes the 'sceptred isle', England, that is being riven by internal strife.

This other Eden, demi-paradise,
This fortress built by Nature for herself
Against infection and the hand of war,
This happy breed of men, this little world,
This precious stone set in the silver sea,
Which serves it in the office of a wall,
Or as a moat defensive to a house,
Against the envy of less happier lands,
This blessed plot, this earth, this realm, this England ...

In the heart of this England runs the river named after the man who wrote those lines, Shakespeare's Avon - a beautiful, uplifting river with a thousand stories to tell.

The Author

Rick Thompson is a former journalist and broadcaster and a lifelong birdwatcher. He worked for BBC News for 27 years, starting at BBC Birmingham where he produced and presented regional wildlife programmes as well as reporting the news. He moved to London where he became a senior editor with BBC Television News and The World Service. Later he returned to the Midlands as the BBC's Head of News, Current Affairs and Local Programmes. Since leaving the BBC, his consultancy, 'T-Media', has organised dozens of training workshops and development projects across the former Communist countries of Europe, helping to promote independent, quality broadcast journalism.

For several years Rick wrote and illustrated a regular column on birds for the Countryside magazine, and for four years he was a member of the Governing Council of the RSPB. He is regularly asked to moderate European conferences on the environment, sustainable energy, biodiversity and climate change.

He says, "I believe that exposure to nature is incredibly important for people's physical and mental well-being, and getting to know more about the natural world is fascinating. A walk beside a river is particularly uplifting, as well as being good exercise. I hope this month-by-month account of a journey through the heart of England beside the Warwickshire

Avon will encourage the reader to get out into the natural environment, and enjoy the changing seasons and the marvellous variety of birds and other creatures that can be found along a river valley.

I also hope you enjoy the stories of the towns along the way, the folklore and legends, and the key moments in England's history that have been played out on the riverbanks. Shakespeare's Avon has many tales to tell that are just as dramatic as the plays written by the Bard.

Other books by this author.
'Park Life' – A Year in the Wildlife of an Urban Park.
Grosvenor House Publishing.
Writing for Broadcast Journalists. Routledge.

Ingram Content Group UK Ltd.
Milton Keynes UK
UKHW041441070623
423034UK00003B/198